Spiritual World 101

A guide to a spiritually happy life

RYUHO OKAWA
IRH Press

Contents

PART ONE

There is Nothing to Fear in Death Once You Know about The Other World

1

What Happens to People After They Die?

2

Let's Learn about the Real State of Heaven and Hell

PART TWO

Gain Knowledge of This World and the Next and Lead A Happy Life

1

How are We Born into This World?

2

Can We Change Our Fate?

3

You are Not Alone in Life

4

You Can Become An Angel Too

PART THREE
How to Protect Yourself Against Negative Spiritual Influences

1
Memorial Services That Can Truly Save The Spirits in the Other World

2
Do Evil Spirits Truly Exist?

PART FOUR

A Correct Understanding of Buddha and God

1

Recognize the Great Love of Buddha and God

2

Faith is Wonderful

Preface

In this book I have described in a simple manner the Truth that is obvious to me in the form of Questions & Answers. In modern terms, this is a guide to a spiritual life and, at the same time, it provides you with an opportunity to understand the true way of life for human beings and what it means to lead a truly happy life. Overall, this book also serves as a rudimentary introduction to religions, written in a way that is easy to understand.

I sincerely hope that this book will bring you the right outlook on life and lead you to a spiritually happy life.

Ryuho Okawa
Founder and CEO of the Happy Science Group
September 2009

You Will Be Happier
If You Believe in the Other World

Have you ever asked yourself which would bring you more happiness: belief or disbelief in the existence of the other world?

Let's say that you are currently 40 years old and that the average lifespan is 80. Then you have another 40 years to live. You will certainly do a number of things over the next 40 years and die at the age of 80. But if you think that after you are cremated, nothing will be left to prove you had a life on earth apart from a handful of ashes and some carbon dioxide, then such thinking can hardly bring you happiness. Surely, you would be much happier if you believed that your soul, your life energy, that led a human life under a particular name, will continue to live on forever, even after you die.

If everything ended with death, then morals, philosophies and religions would all be meaningless. What would be the point of improving your character? What reason would there be for studying, working hard or making the effort to create good interpersonal relationships? Why put all your effort into living?

If death put an end to everything, then life would be truly meaningless. There would be no point in improving your character, in making an effort, devoting yourself to study or aiming to improve your character. Only con artists would recommend that you do so. Even though you may succeed in gaining status, income and an earthly form of happiness by improving your character, if everything ends with death, then these are quite meaningless. Which way of thinking do you think will lead to true happiness?

If you believe that the knowledge and abilities you have struggled to acquire in this world can be taken with you to the world after death and that your character will continue to exist in the next world, then surely your efforts now will seem more meaningful; your exertions will appear more wonderful.

The question is whether to believe that everything ends with death or to believe that your character will remain after death and that if you make as much effort as you can, you will be able to continue wonderful activities even after you have died. Which do you want to bet on? Which belief will bring you greater happiness?

As I will explain in this book, I have absolute proof of the existence of the world after death. There can be no doubt that betting on the existence of a world after death will allow you to live a happier life.

I want you to decide for yourself which way of thinking will bring the greatest happiness, to accept what should be accepted and to study the knowledge of Truth rationally. I believe this is most important.

Once you know about the true world, and once you understand that the way you live your life will decide which realm you go to after death, at the very least, you will no longer need to fear the world after death.

There is Nothing to Fear
In Death Once You Know
About the Other World

[Chapter 1]

What Happens to People
After They Die?

What Happens at
The Moment of Death?

Ordinary people find it very difficult
To realize their own death

When the physical body dies, human beings do not disappear. The soul resides within the physical body and when the physical body dies, the soul leaves the body and returns to the other world.

Usually, however, people do not easily recognize their own death. There are some who leave their bodies swiftly the same day they die, but many others do not recognize that they have died. They remain inside their bodies for a while, continuing to feel ill as they did before dying. Consequently, the following can happen: When people hear others around them say that they are dead, they may think, "What are they talking about, I'm still alive!" Someone may open their eyelids and shine light into their eyes, making them say, "That's too bright!" Then they hear someone say, "There is no response. The pupils are already dilated" or "The heart has stopped beating," even though they can still feel their heart beating.

They may think, "That's strange. My heart is still beating. This doctor has misdiagnosed my condition! He said my brain waves have also stopped but my brain is still working perfectly!" In this way, the dead usually continue to believe that they are still alive. They feel especially confused because their spiritual self still retains the form of their physical body.

They first begin to realize that they are dead Upon witnessing their own funeral

Soon they hear their own death being announced and their families begin to cry. They may say, "Why are you crying now? If you felt this way, I wish you could have shown these feelings before." However, people around them do not seem to hear what they say. They also feel strange because they cannot move their bodies.

Later that day, many people come to a wake and prepare for the funeral. At this point, if the dead have some knowledge of life after death, they could begin to think that they may have died but are not quite sure. If they have no knowledge of life after death, they still believe that they are alive and suspect everyone else has gone mad.

When the wake or funeral begins, the dead may see their own picture or coffin on display and say, "Come on! Please stop this nonsense! I don't want to die yet."

The silver cord connecting the soul And body will break

During this time, the soul repeatedly leaves and re-enters the body. The dead remain in their own house for a while, sometimes floating toward the ceiling or roof. But they look down, get scared and quickly return to their bodies.

Human beings have a "silver cord," a very fine thread that stretches from the back of the head, which connects the soul and the body. As long as it does not break, the soul can return to the body. If it is broken, the soul can never return to the original body.

True death does not occur when the physical body stops functioning. This usually takes place about one day after physical death.

What is a Silver Cord?

The true moment of death:

Once the silver cord is broken, the soul is no longer able to return to the physical body. The true moment of death is when the silver cord breaks. Generally speaking, it takes about 24 hours after the heart stops for the silver cord to break.

Silver cord:

The body and the soul are connected by a silver cord.

Soul

Body

From ancient times, the existence of the silver cord has been known in different places around the world. There is a description of the silver cord in the Old Testament as well as in some books in the age of Socrates. In Japan, the silver cord has traditionally been referred to as the "cord of a soul."

There are people who do not wish To die and try to resist

The process may take longer if the dead person cannot easily accept his death and is furiously resisting it. Sometimes a corpse becomes so stiff with rigor mortis that it cannot be bent to fit inside the coffin. This is sign that the soul is resisting, saying, "I don't want to die. I won't go inside the coffin no matter what." This is quite a difficult situation. Some people remain furious even after their bodies have been cremated. They return home and complain to their families, saying, "You are all so cold-hearted. Are you that happy to know that I'm dead? You should have taken better care of me." However, their families cannot hear what they are saying.

Some people accept their death but do not like the way their funeral is handled. They may complain about the ceremony or the sum of money spent.

What Kind of Things
Do We Experience
After Our Spirit Leaves the Body?

Your spirit lingers in this world
For about three weeks after death

Spirits of dead people must leave this world within 49 days after they die. Actually, there is a general rule that they should not remain wandering on earth for more than about three weeks after death. They must leave after about 49 days at the longest. Up until that time, they are left to do as they like. They are not yet ready to enter the other world completely, so they travel back and forth between this world and the next. They wander around and watch the people in this world. They are concerned about how their funeral is proceeding, how their properties are being passed on, how their companies are being managed, whether their children are getting along well or whether their spouses are seeing other men and women. So they linger in this world for almost two months. After this period, however, they are told that it's time to leave.

Actually, when a person dies, a spirit or guide comes and takes him to the next world but he tends to return to this world once again. The person is permitted to stay here for a while in order to study the differences between the next world and this one. As time passes, he becomes accustomed to being a spirit and his physical or materialistic attributes gradually drop away. Around this time, he is suggested to leave this world and enter the next.

Crossing the Styx

Eventually, the spirits of dead people will come to the Styx. Once they have passed over this river, they will truly become dead to this world. Then they arrive at the entrance to the Spirit World or what is referred to as the Astral or Posthumous Realm.

On the opposite bank of the Styx, they usually see a vast field full of rape blossoms and other beautiful flowers and they will find deceased relatives, friends and various other people welcoming them. Many of them believe that they have arrived in Heaven. This is not exactly Heaven, however; it is the Astral Realm. The Astral Realm is a place where spirits first go to after death and wait until it is determined whether they will go to Heaven or Hell.

*The final destination is dictated by
The spirit's self-reflection on his life*

They also spend a while in that realm and live as spirits, reflecting on their lives before their final destinations are decided. During this period, they are shown their whole life in the form of a movie or a guiding spirit may come to discuss various events that happened in their life, one at a time.

Since we have movies in the world today, people's lives are often presented as a kind of movie in the next world. Sometimes people's life is displayed in a kind of mirror. In the old days, when people did not yet know of screen images, they were apparently presented with a notebook in which all deeds during their life on earth were listed. In Buddhist and Hindu countries, this notebook is called the "Records of Yama," Yama being the supreme judge in Hell.

The scientist, philosopher and mystic Emanuel Swedenborg [1688-1772], who left a vast amount of written material regarding the Spirit World based on his experiences, reports having seen the following:

"A spirit was called for its turn to repent the deeds

he carried out in life. When he was on earth, this man had received bribes and done illegal transactions, all of which he kept a close record of in a little notebook. As the judge spirit stared at his face and his entire body, the notebook he had written suddenly came out of the ground and, at his feet, the pages fluttered open allowing all the other spirits there to see what he had done.

"This notebook even contained records of things that the man had forgotten he had done. It listed everything that the man had thought and done while he was alive on earth and, as the pages turned, the other spirits were able to see his thoughts and deeds. What is more, there were even things that he had never written. He was so surprised and shocked."

In the old days, this was the way the spirits of dead people saw the details of their lives. When they reflected on their past thoughts and deeds, sometimes these records appeared in written form. But today, it is much more common for people's lives to be presented in the form of a movie or as images in a mirror. After having, in the Astral Realm, reflected on their life, their destination in the next world will finally be decided.

What You Will Experience After Death

3 **_Reflect on your entire life:_**
Your entire life will be shown on something like a movie screen. After you have reflected on your thoughts and deeds in your lifetime, your destination in the other world will be determined.

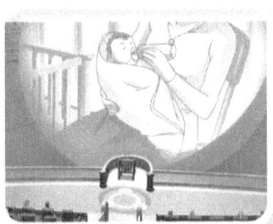

2 **_Cross the Styx:_**
Eventually a spirit will come to guide you on your departure to the other world and you will cross the Styx.

1 **_Prepare for departure to the other world:_**
For about three weeks after death, you will observe your families and other people on earth whom you are concerned about.

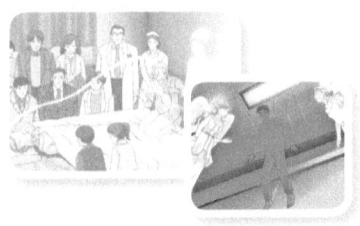

From the movie, _The Laws of Eternity_
Ryuho Okawa, 2006

Do You Still Experience Hunger and Sleep Even After Becoming a Spirit?

Essentially people have no appetite In the other world

After you have returned to the other world you will have no physical body, so there is no need to eat. Some of the inhabitants in the fourth and fifth dimensions retain the habit of eating but they do so merely to enjoy the sensation of eating. They do not actually consume food.

When they are entertaining or talking they feel that something is missing, so they eat and drink. But they do not actually get full in a physical sense. In other words, appetite, which is one of the three great desires of this world, does not actually exist in the other world.

The source of energy in the other world is the Spiritual Sun. The spirits there live on spiritual energy that comes from the Spiritual Sun. For this reason, appetite, a desire so powerful in this world, essentially does not exist in the next.

The spirits in the other world are active all day

Next, I would like to talk about sleep. In this world, it is preferable to sleep about eight hours a day. On the other hand, the spirits in the next world do not sleep. It is always daytime there, so they do not sleep.

Of course, emotionally, they may sometimes feel like "resting their bodies," but sleep itself no longer exists in the other world. While it is always night in Hell, it is always daytime in Heaven. Therefore, although the spirits of Heaven may spend time relaxing, they are not actually sleeping.

While you are living in a physical body, food and sleep are both impossible to do without but once you lose the body, such things are no longer necessary. If you continue to experience these desires for a long time even after you die, it means you either believe that the flesh to be the master and the spirit its servant or that the flesh is all you are.

Do You Still Age Even After Becoming a Spirit?

In the Spirit World, You can take on any appearance you desire

Naturally, the vast majority of dead people are old. If they were all to retain the same consciousness as at the moment of death, it would result in the other world becoming an old people's Heaven. This would lead to old people's homes all around and it would make the scenery there quite different to the way we usually think of Heaven. This is not to say that is a bad thing but it certainly would not look the way it is generally depicted.

In fact, after people leave this world, they go through a period during which they get rid of earthly attributes. This period differs from person to person: some will complete it in an extremely short period, about three days, or even return directly to the realm they originally came from. But on average, it takes about three years. For approximately three years people go to some place where they undergo spiritual training to cleanse themselves of the impurities they accumulated on earth.

In this process, they become aware of the true essence of the soul. After that, their guardian or guiding spirit* will teach them what it means to be a spiritual being. At the same time, they will also learn that in the Spirit World they can change their appearance at will and they will study this through actual experience.

For instance, once they think of what they would like to wear, those clothes will appear. They will learn by experiencing these things for themselves. It generally takes about three years in worldly time to master this concept.

Once they master it, they are able to adopt any form they like. Those who like to look old will adopt an aged appearance while those who prefer to look young will do that.

---

* A guardian spirit is a spirit in charge of protecting a person on earth. Each person on earth is assigned one guardian spirit (refer to page 80 of this book). A guiding spirit is usually a spirit which is of a higher spiritual level than a guardian spirit and is mainly in charge of guiding the person on earth with regard to his work.

What Happens After Death to People Who Commit Suicide?

They either become earthbound spirits Or fall to Hell

The answer is that they do not all necessarily go to Hell; the majority will find themselves in Hell or at the stage just before it. While some people go immediately to Hell, many do not even go there. Being unable to understand that they are dead and retaining their attachments to their life on earth, they carry on living in much the same way as people who are still alive or they become earthbound spirits and wander around in places such as the place of their death.

In this way, they still stick to the people and things of this world, and are incapable of even moving on to Hell. If they did go to Hell, their suffering would surface more clearly, of course, but many of them are unable to move on to that stage.

Then, is it absolutely impossible for those who commit suicide to enter Heaven? No, that is not necessarily the case. If we look at Japanese history, for instance, there is Takamori Saigo who was the leader of the revolt against the newly formed Meiji government in the 19th century. Upon seeing the failure of the revolt, he committed *seppuku*, so in the end he took his own life. Another example is that of a general of the Imperial Japanese Army, Maresuke Nogi. He committed suicide following the death of Emperor Meiji. However, neither of them is in Hell now. They doubtless suffered when they died but returned to the heavenly world and became gods after that.

The main reasons they did not fall to Hell were that, while they were alive, they had pure minds and were adored by large numbers of people. In this way, sometimes there are cases where other principles work.

People who commit suicide as a form of escape Will not return to Heaven

This being said, however, in most cases when a person commits suicide as a means of escaping from this world, it is very rare for him to enter Heaven immediately; this scarcely ever happens. It is extremely difficult for people to enter Heaven right after they die without the knowledge of the Real World. Even if angels come and try to explain the situation to them, they cannot accept what they are being told. People who did not listen to the advice of others in this world will most likely display the same behavior in the other world.

The Post-death Situation of Those Who Commit Suicide

Among people who have committed suicide there are many who do not realize that they are already dead. For example, somebody who hanged himself may continue hanging himself numerous times even after he is dead. As he still believes that he is unable to die, he then goes on to possess people who are still alive, causing them to hang themselves. In this way, he relives the moment of death numerous times.

If the person was born into this world with a mission to live until 80 but commits suicide at 50, he will be unable to enter either Heaven or Hell for 30 years after death.

There is Nothing to Fear In Death Once You Know About the Other World

[Chapter 2]

Let's Learn About the Real State Of Heaven and Hell

What Does the Other World Look Like?

The other world coexists with this one

Let me now present you with an overview of the other world, that is to say, the Spirit World. While there are many ways to explain the Spirit World, to put it in a broader context, it is the world where people go after they leave this earthly world. In other words, it is the place where people's souls go after their bodies have died.

This being said, I do not want you to think of the Spirit World as a place that exists above the clouds. This is an important point. I would like you to know that the Spirit World actually coexists here in the same space we are now occupying.

Of course, it is often explained that the Spirit World is divided into many levels, high and low, or that it feels as if the realms of high spirits exist thousands or tens of thousands of feet above the earth. However, these are just figurative expressions used to describe the Spirit World in a way that people on earth are able to understand.

In fact, the very basis for the existence of the Spirit World is that it coexists with this material world. Therefore, I want you to think of the Spirit World as being something that exists here, simultaneous with the world in which we live, rather than something that exists a vast distance away.

It is very similar to the situation where invisible radio waves are constantly transmitted in this world. For example, each channel on T.V. shows a variety of different images and the radio waves corresponding to these images are transmitted through the world. The Spirit World resembles the world of these radio waves. Since its wavelengths and frequencies differ from those of this world, a different world is created. So the fact is that it does not exist in a completely different place.

In other words, as with T.V., if you have a device that receives the wavelengths of the Spirit World, sometimes it would show the world of Hell, sometimes the world of Heaven and yet other times the scenery of the world of high spirits.

The other world consists of multiple dimensions

One of the important points in the teachings of Happy Science concerning the Spirit World is that we explain clearly the concept of "dimensions."

In the fields of physics and mathematics, it has been made clear that in the environment surrounding Earth, there exist not only the three-dimensional world in which we live — the world that consists of the three axes of length, width and height — but also a four-dimensional space that contains an additional axis of "time," a world that consists of length, width, height and time. It has also been made clear that beyond such a world, there exist the worlds of the fifth, sixth, seventh, eighth and ninth dimensions as well. However, scientists can only understand their existence as scientific theory. They have no clear idea about what kind of worlds these really are.

I have conducted research into the Spirit World in various ways and, as a result, it became clear that the worlds corresponding to these dimensions, which physics has speculated on, do actually exist.

The fourth dimension is the world that people go to immediately after death. It is known as the Posthumous Realm and within it, in its lower depths, is the place known as Hell while the upper reaches are known as the Astral Realm.

Above this is the Realm of Goodness. This is the fifth dimension and it is a world that is populated by good-hearted people.

Then comes the sixth dimension, which is called the Realm of Light. In this realm, divine spirits reside and the prominent among them are sometimes worshipped as saints by those who are living on earth. It is a world where specialists in every field come together and it is also the place where the high spirits with a special mission live.

Above the Realm of Light is what is known in Buddhism as the Realm of Bodhisattvas. This is a world inhabited by those whose main focus is to help others or, put in another way, to perform acts of love. They have very few worries about themselves. All they are concerned with is saving or guiding as many people as possible. Spirits that are an embodiment of such love reside in the Realm of Bodhisattvas in the seventh dimension.

The eighth dimension is the Realm of Tathagatas. This is a world inhabited by the founders of worldwide religions, great philosophers, great statesmen and other magnificent people who acted as central figures in shaping the history of different eras.

The ninth dimension is the highest level where human spirits can reside and is known as the Cosmic Realm or Realm of the Saviors. Shakyamuni Buddha,

Jesus Christ, Moses and other spirits who are referred to as "Grand Tathagatas" belong here. This is the place inhabited by those who come down to earth once every few thousand years to teach fundamental philosophies and launch grand civilizations.

I have given more detailed information about the structure of the dimensions in my books of theorized teachings — *The Laws of the Sun* [New York: IRH Press, 2013] Chapter One and *The Nine Dimensions* [New York: IRH Press, 2012]. In *The Nine Dimensions* in particular, I have explained each dimension in detail in a separate chapter, for example, the first chapter is entitled, "The World of the Fourth Dimension," the second chapter "The World of the Fifth Dimension" and so on, so please refer to it to learn more.

Dimensional Structure in The Other World

Ninth Dimension – Cosmic Realm:
Realm of the Saviors

Eighth Dimension – Realm of Tathagatas:
Realm of spirits who were central figures
in shaping the history of different eras

Seventh Dimension – Realm of Bodhisattvas:
Realm of spirits whose main focus is to help
others

Sixth Dimension – Realm of Light:
Realm of specialists and divine spirits

Fifth Dimension – Realm of Goodness:
Realm of good-hearted spirits

Fourth Dimension – Posthumous Realm:
Realm where people go to immediately
after death

Hell

Hell is not equal
in size to Heaven;
it exists in the
lower part of the
Posthumous Realm.

Third Dimension – Earthly Realm

Minor Heaven – Sennin and Tengu Realms

What is the Minor Heaven In the Spirit World?

The Magician, Sennin [Hermit Sorcerers] And Tengu [Goblin] Realms

In the Spirit World, there are not only differences on the vertical level but also on the horizontal plane. To be more precise, there is the Major Heaven where spirits who have achieved spiritual growth and evolved in an orthodox direction reside, as well as the Minor Heaven inhabited by magicians, sennin and tengu.*

A good example of the Minor Heaven is the world of *Harry Potter*. Several movies have been made in this series, so you may have watched them or read the books.

While the world of magic is fun to read about, when it appears in movies, there are lots of scenes that are quite eerie. But this is not to say that the realm is entirely a part of Hell. While it is indeed one of the realms

---

* *Sennin* are fond of psychic powers, magic and spiritual phenomena and are always involved with these matters. *Tengu* like to boast of their powers or wisdom.

of the other world, it is different from the crystal-clear world of spirits that I usually teach about. This is a place where many eerie, uncanny and fantastic events occur; it is a kind of magical world.

The appearances and words of the high spirits described in Happy Science are of the sort that we would expect; how great figures on earth would appear and what they would say if they had continued to evolve in the next world. On the other hand, *Harry Potter* describes a mysterious and weird world where the characters cast spells on one another.

In Japan, we have the movies by Hayao Miyazaki, which deal with similar kinds of realms. His *Spirited Away* [2001] and *Princess Mononoke* [1997] depict many scenes from the Magician, Sennin and Tengu Realms. While the Japanese Spirit World and the Scottish Spirit World are different, the worlds of Miyazaki and *Harry Potter* have a very similar atmosphere. These are what are referred to as the Minor Heaven.

In Japan, there was a man named Onisaburo Deguchi, who founded the Omoto religion and was active during the first half of the 20th century. He originally came from the Minor Heaven. He published a book entitled, *Reikai Monogatari* [Tales of the Spirit World] in which he described his travels through various realms in the Spirit World. While this is an old book and difficult to read, it contains stories of numerous fantastic worlds that are just like those depicted in *Harry Potter* or Miyazaki's films. There are numerous stories of foxes or raccoon dogs that bewitch each other, worlds where snakes suddenly appear and worlds in constant change where creatures transform themselves into a variety of shapes.

Happy Science has published two volumes of spiritual messages from Onisaburo Deguchi [*Okawa Ryuho Reigen Zenshu, 46, 49,* (A Collection of Spiritual Messages by Ryuho Okawa, Vols. 46 and 49) (Tokyo: Happy Science, 2008 and 2009)] and, for the most part, these deal with the Minor Heaven. These are about the kind of world where the inhabitants fight with psychic powers using magic, trying to transform their opponents into different forms. There is actually a world that is based around magic.

What Kind of Place is Hell?

A place where people with strong attachments to The earthly world will go

There are probably a lot of people who think of Hell as being a world that just appears in fairy tales, a world depicted in Buddhist scrolls or a special place created by Christianity for educational purposes. However, Hell actually does exist. Although this fact may be extremely difficult to accept, such a world really does exist.

Hell is a world that exists extremely close to the earthly world. Of course, those in Hell no longer have physical bodies nor do they belong to this world. But they attach very strongly to the earthly world and are unable to purify themselves as souls. To put it another way, they still have not fully awakened to the fact that they are spirits.

If you listen to the conversations of the inhabitants of Hell, you will find that the vast majority of them do not even understand that they are already dead. Some of them do know that they are dead but, in most cases, they do not understand what is going on, where they are now, what they should do next or what they did wrong.

There are numerous stages in Hell

Hell comprises numerous stages, ranging from the upper to the lower ones, each corresponding to the vibrations of the mind. For example, in the relatively upper stages of Hell there is the *Asura* Hell which is inhabited by souls who have led a life of fighting and destruction, as well as the Hell of Lust inhabited by souls who have gone wrong on the path of man-woman relationship while they were alive. There is also a realm for souls who have lived by crime, for instance, cheating, killing, injuring, robbing others and so on. This realm contains further different stages according to the level of the crimes.

In the lowest level of Hell is the Unfathomable Hell where those who have taught false ideologies or religions, misleading many and destroying people's lives, go after death. In the world of spirits, the act of deluding the souls of others is considered the greatest crime, much worse than acts of physical wrongdoings such as murder or crimes, or mistakes at the material level.

In addition, there is the Demon Realm that originated centered around Unfathomable Hell, where Satan and other devils reside.

Hell does not exist simply as a punishment

The important point to note is that Hell is not simply a place where you are punished for your sins. It is an undeniable fact that Hell is a world to which souls betake themselves in accordance with the tendencies of their own mind. In other words, because a soul emits coarse vibrations which act as a form of heavy sediment, it is unable to rise to the upper levels and instead sinks to the depths. This is the reason explained in terms of physical science.

In moral terms, it can be said that after death, each person reflects on his thoughts and deeds during his lifetime in the light of his own conscience. If he finds that he is unable to forgive himself, he will choose to go to the world of Hell and undertake further soul training.

It is impossible to be reborn into
This world directly from Hell

One point that must not be overlooked here is the fact that while people's souls are reborn into this world through a process of reincarnation, it is not possible to reincarnate directly from Hell. This is not something that is stressed in conventional religions and many people are ignorant of it. But the truth is that souls cannot be reborn into this world from Hell.

Since the spirits in Hell are unable to be born here, they try to possess people on earth and make them suffer. This is the phenomenon of spiritual possession that they cause. If they could be reborn from where they are, they could be born again in a physical body, thereby escaping the torments of Hell. But since this is impossible, they possess living people and delude them in an effort to escape from Hell's agony.

In any case, the inhabitants of Hell led lives filled with thoughts and deeds that went against the Will of Buddha. They are required to undertake deep self-reflection on this point.

Mini Column 2

Can Souls that Fall To Hell Return to Heaven?

Even with evil spirits, as they advance in their practice of self-reflection to some extent, light will appear from the back of the head on their pitch-black spirit body. When they repent and say, "I was wrong" with tears running down their cheeks, these will wash away the soot-like dirt that has built up on their spirit body, allowing light to shine forth. Then, after they truly reflect deep enough into their heart, they will rise to the heavenly world.

What Kind of People Fall to Hell?

People who have the three poisons Of the mind are in danger

The main causes of people falling to Hell are greed, anger and foolishness, which are the three poisons of the mind.

1) Greed—a covetous heart

Greed refers to a covetous and avaricious heart. In the terminology of Happy Science, it means people who live by "taking love." Nearly all of the people who live taking love or live with an avaricious heart will go to Hell.

The characteristic of people with greed is that they, themselves, do not realize they are being greedy, when in fact it is quite obvious to other people. Those around them say, "He is a greedy and insatiable person. He doesn't understand other people's feelings at all," or "He is always taking things and only thinks about what he can get." And nine out of ten people will agree that it is true. But often, the individual concerned does not realize this. Thus, it is very difficult to see oneself correctly.

To overcome this insatiable greed, it is extremely important that you learn how to be content. You should also nurture the spirit of offering. Religions often recommend making donations because this teaches people to give. By giving, you can get rid of attachments.

People who are always concerned with what they can get for themselves do not think of giving to others or making an offering to a holy cause. If they had the spirit of offering, they would not be condemned to Hell for the sin of greed. But since they never think of anything but personal gain, they are in Hell.

2) Anger—a raging heart

There are people who are prone to fly into a rage and in most cases this is due to feelings of dissatisfaction. When things do not go as they wish, they fly into a rage out of discontent.

Among members of your family who have died, such as your grandfather, grandmother, father or mother, if there are some whom you remember as being short-tempered, quickly flying into a rage and venting their anger on those around them, then there is a high possibility that they have gone to Hell because of it.

3) Foolishness—an ignorant heart

Ignorance means foolishness, but it does not necessarily mean "unintelligent." There are many who are considered clever when it comes to the things of this world but who can nevertheless be considered foolish. What ignorance means is not knowing the Truth. People who are ignorant of the Truth do appear foolish.

Through the eyes of somebody who understands the Truth, a lot of people waste their energy on things that are quite irrelevant or opposite to the Truth; they are desperately trying to do things that actually dig their own grave. Still, in worldly terms, they are often very clever people. So there are actually people whose efforts only serve to expand the region of Hell. This kind of foolishness does exist.

If you gain the knowledge of the Truth while you are still alive, you will not fall to Hell. But because people do not gain that knowledge, they end up going there.

What Do I Have to Do to Return To Heaven After Death?

Live your life with a smile on your face

Heaven is usually said to be filled with brilliant light. It is sometimes called the world of perpetual bliss or everlasting summer. It could be called the world of joy. If I were to describe it in an earthly way, I would say Heaven is like a place where close friends get together and enjoy talking with one another.

The most distinctive characteristic of the inhabitants of Heaven is, in a word, innocence. They are artless and pure. They have hearts of gold, the basic requirement for living in Heaven. The inhabitants of Heaven are always willing to be gentle to others and at the same time willing to do what is truly good for themselves. They do good because of a desire to spread happiness around them, rather than causing others harm.

If I were to make a summary of the minimum requirements for living in Heaven, one would be that you are able to always live with a smile on your face; not a superficial smile but a natural smile. The inhabitants of Heaven live like this.

Therefore, when you practice self-reflection, if you cannot determine what it is that you must correct, I would like to suggest that you do a simple mental exercise: imagine that you have no social status, position or reputation that you can rely on. Then think honestly whether you would still have a natural smile on your face.

Love many people and be liked by many people

Another point to consider is that basically no one in Heaven was disliked by many when living on earth. This may sound simplistic, but it is quite true that Heaven is a place where people that others like live. Those people who are liked by others are actually the ones who have liked others. It is a rule that people who like others are also liked by them.

If you wish to return to Heaven, you have to be someone who is sincere, who always has a smile on his face and who gives love to many and is liked by many. If you cannot satisfy these simple requirements, the door of Heaven will not open for you.

What I am trying to say is that those whose presence makes others uncomfortable cannot live in Heaven.

You must live with a pure heart

Heaven is a place where everything you think about is transparent as if others can see through your mind. So if you entertain evil thoughts, you cannot live there in harmony with others as if you are a part of a flock of sheep grazing peacefully together. One way of describing the reality of Heaven is that it is a place inhabited by those who feel no shame in exposing what they think. Those whose minds are full of vile thoughts, thoughts that are poisonous and evil, will not be allowed to live in Heaven because of the evilness.

I would like you to reflect deeply on whether you can expose what you think publicly, without hesitation or shame. If you feel you have to hide this or that, you should know that Heaven is still far away.

For a human being, the ideal life is to live appreciated and thought highly of by both others and yourself, while living candidly, innocently and simply. Living in Heaven is no more difficult than that.

The Reason Why We Cannot See The Other World or Spirits

It is not easy to convince people of the world after death. Besides, as a structure of the world, it is true that it is made in such a way that it cannot be completely proven.

If it were possible to see the other world with our own eyes, then everybody would believe in its existence. However, what if everybody could experience that our world and the other coexist and see that, in this world, many spirits are actually walking around in the same space as living people? Would it be possible for mortal people and spirits to live together? It would certainly be very difficult.

Imagine, for example, that the spirits of the other world talked to you. Whenever you harbor a question in your mind, you would soon get an answer from the spirits. You are always being told what you should do by the spirits. If you were living in such a world, you would have a really tough time.

I, myself, actually live in this sort of world but it requires strenuous efforts to keep my mind from taking off. It would be unbearable for ordinary people; they would be regarded as mad for saying strange things and, in most cases, they would be sent into isolation.

It requires a lot of strength to be able to live a normal life while experiencing the other world. Unless you have a highly developed rational sense and intellect, you would most likely go insane. Living every day in contact with the Spirit World, your thoughts and actions would become distorted and very few people are able to withstand this.

When your mind is open to the spiritual world, there is no problem as long as you are being led by good spirits, but you are also susceptible to bad ones. If evil spirits or those that are malicious come to possess you, you will feel their presence directly and begin to hear their voices. Then it would be practically impossible for you to continue living as a normal person and you would most likely end up destroying your life.

It is only in a world like that of the movie, *Ghostbusters*, where people can still do their work despite being able to see and feel the world of spirits. The work of "ghost hunters" is to chase down ghosts, so people are able to do that. There are also professional psychics who make it their business to deal with spirits.

In the case of ordinary people, however, if they develop spiritual abilities to the level where they can completely prove the existence of the world of spirits as something real, they will then be unable to lead a normal life.

For example, in circumstances where your dead grandparents and parents are always watching you in your room or come to talk to you at night when you are in bed, you would be unable to live normally. So it is much better not to be able to see the spirits nor hear their voices.

Gain Knowledge of This World and the Next and Lead A Happy Life

[Chapter 1]

How are We Born into This World?

Do Reincarnation and Past Lives Really Exist?

Human beings have eternal life and Are reborn countless times

I have repeatedly taught that the other world really does exist and that it is the true home of humans. I have also said, time and again, that the few decades we spend on earth are merely a fleeting dream, nothing more than a temporary journey.

Human beings have eternal, imperishable life. As souls, we have lived through thousands, tens of thousands of years, or even longer. During this period, we are allowed to undergo soul training, over and over again, residing in the physical body given to us by our parents, which serves as a vehicle to carry our soul, and experiencing our descendants' flourishing.

*It is wonderful to be able to experience
Different cultures and civilizations*

There are probably people who ask, "Why do we have to go through such a complicated system?" or who wonder, "Surely it would be better for us simply to continue our lives in the Spirit World. Why do we have to be born into this world in a physical body and experience the journey down the river of life, if we are only going to die eventually and return to the other world?"

As somebody who has actually experienced the truth, I will describe the secret of reincarnation in an easy-to-understand way by stating, "Reincarnation is actually the ultimate system for achieving happiness that Buddha created."

During the decades that we inhabit a physical body on earth, we have an individual name and live our life to the best of our ability, thinking, "I am a unique being who has the name, *so-and-so*." But viewed from the perspective of our memories of a long, long span of reincarnations, we will realize that our name represents no more than a role we take for a brief period in a particular theater of life. You will come to understand the fact that people take part in plays on different stages, in different eras, playing the roles of actors who have different names as they develop their performance skills.

Although you may be living as Japanese at the moment, you could have been Chinese in a previous era. Or you might have been British, American or French. In the past, you may have lived in India or Egypt.

Please imagine this possibility in your mind. Surely you will feel what a wonderful experience it may be, what a wonderful world it is.

You are born into various civilizations where different cultures flourish. You grow up, work, love, marry, raise children, age and eventually die. Although aging and death are very sad, by passing through them you will be given another new opportunity.

Can Humans Be Reincarnated As Animals?

Basically, humans always reincarnate as humans

Humans always reincarnate as humans, except in very rare cases where a human soul experiences a life as an animal for a brief period for the purpose of special training. This occurs only in the bodies of highly evolved animals and only for a period of one or two years. This kind of special training is arranged to teach people how precious it is to be born as human beings. It means that some domestic animals like dogs and cats may have been human in the past. And since they still possess human senses, living in an animal body is an excruciating experience. When such difficult life is over, these souls will have realized how wonderful it is to be human. But as I said earlier, this only occurs rarely and as an exception.

What is Karma?

It is the homework that each soul carries with him

The soul begins to develop certain inclinations through repeated reincarnations. As a person repeats life on earth, his soul begins to show distinctly its strengths and weaknesses.

As a result of studying the system of reincarnation in detail, I have found that before coming to this world, human beings clearly determine the theme of their soul training in this lifetime.

After having experienced several lives on earth, if one has failed to overcome a certain problem, he will be tested again under similar or quite opposite circumstances to see whether or not he can resolve the problem.

Male souls often reincarnate as males while female souls often reincarnate as females. However, I have ascertained that at times the sexes change. Suppose there is a man who oppresses and abuses his wife, making her question why she must lead such a miserable life. Then the man returns to the other world with the so-called karma or assignment that his soul is burdened with.

Is there a way to redeem karma?

He will redeem his karma in one of two ways. One way is to marry again or have a relationship with a similar female soul under similar circumstances.

There, he is tested to see if he will abuse the woman in the same way as before or will transform himself and lead a harmonious, married life or have a friendly relationship with her. The other option would be to be born as a woman and experience being abused by a man. These are the two extreme cases of redeeming one's karma. He may be tested repeatedly, under either similar circumstances or completely different circumstances where he will be abused instead of being the abuser.

Some of you may be physically disabled, which is quite heartbreaking if you only consider the present lifetime. However, life reading reveals that 80 to 90 percent of the causes of physical disabilities are to be found in past lives.

In past incarnations, human beings have experienced much violence; for instance, fighting and war. In that process, if a person ever injured someone else in some way, he will feel pain in the same part of his own body because of his karma.

For example, there are people who were born as Romans in past lives and injured the eyes of others, e.g. poking out or pushing in people's eyeballs. These people might have difficulty with their eyes in their next incarnation. Others might have trouble with their ears.

Likewise, if a person went to war and injured the legs of another with a sword, he may be born physically disabled in one of his next incarnations. Thus, humans are often given another chance to redeem their karma since their foolishness keeps them from understanding the pain of others unless they feel it themselves.

Redeeming karma is not merely a punishment

Furthermore, there are also some who not only repeat the opposite situation as punishment but also voluntarily put themselves into such circumstances. Although they have fully repented for the mistakes they made on earth, they cannot forgive themselves or cannot help having a guilty conscience and choose to live in a difficult situation. They might ask, "Please let me be born into these particular circumstances to improve my soul." They cannot forgive themselves no matter how much they reflect, so they say, "Please let me have this sort of experience once again."

For example, there are people whose carelessness caused the loss of their children or loved ones. Try as they may, they cannot bear the guilt. So when they are born again, they ask, "Please put me in circumstances where I cannot complete the natural span of my life. I would like to experience this." And they are born sickly or are killed in an accident at an early age.

Placed in such a situation, some may consider it to be their misfortune, forgetting that it was planned before they were born and hold grudges against their parents, friends, teachers, environment or country. But they are mistaken.

Part 2

Gain Knowledge of This World and the Next and Lead A Happy Life

[Chapter 2]

Can We Change Our Fate?

Is Fate Predetermined And Unchangeable?

There is a certain flexibility in one's fate

If you ask me whether fate is unchangeable, the answer is that there are also parts of fate which can be changed. While there are parts of human fate that are predetermined and unchangeable, there is a lot of latitude for change which is left to the discretion of individual free will. The extent of this discretion varies according to the individual.

What are the factors that constitute human fate?

First, there is the life plan that each individual created before birth.

Second, there is the degree of personal endeavor the individual exhibits after birth.

Third, there are spiritual influences which include those of the individual's guardian and guiding spirits, as well as those of evil spirits such as haunting spirits.

It is a combination of these factors that decides the fate of an individual.

Is there any proof that fate is not fixed?

One thing that I would like you to consider here is that nobody plans to fall to Hell before they are born into this world. Although some may feel that could be the result in a worst-case scenario, they are born believing it is most unlikely to come to that.

However, the truth is that quite a large number of people actually end up in Hell. We can say that their fate has largely changed between the time they were born and the time they die. This change has taken place as a result of the second factor, which is personal endeavor, and the third factor, spiritual influences.

If you are able to receive the guidance of your guardian spirit and lead a good life, there is no problem. However, if you create darkness in your mind and live with a misguided heart, you will be possessed by evil spirits, causing your mind to turn in an ever heavier and darker direction until finally, you fall to Hell.

Is A Person's Lifespan Fixed?

If a person has a reason to exist in this world, It is possible for his life to be extended

It is said that the span of a person's life is already fixed but this is not 100 percent true. In fact, you can actually extend your life by your efforts.

In the course of your life, you come to several turning points which mark the start of new phases; these are, to a certain degree, prearranged. There are many turning points, for example, at 55, 70, 75, 80 years old and so on.

If you are able to achieve some sort of revolution in your thinking at these turning points, you may be able to extend your own life.

If you can offer some reason why you should remain in this world, you can extend your life here. If you are unable to do this, you have to leave. But if you can demonstrate some reason for your continued presence, you will be allowed to remain here. So if you wish to live longer, you need to have some reason for your continued presence. The most common reason is that you still have work to do, so you should make plans for your future. Please have such thoughts in your mind.

If I were to give advice to those who think they do not have much longer to live, it would be this: "Please go ahead and make a plan to live to 120." If you decide you are going to live to this age, you will find that most of your worries disappear. You will know exactly what you have to do and you can set about accomplishing it little by little. It is important to go ahead, regardless of whether or not your life will end during that process.

Does the "Red String of Fate" Really Exist?

In the other world, people promise to Get married before they are born

In principle, most people make a promise to get married before they are born.

For the average soul, the period between incarnations is approximately 300 years. High spirits have a much longer span; the souls of bodhisattvas are born into this world once every 700 to 800 years, whereas the souls of tathagatas are born once every 1,000 to 2,000 years. While people are reborn countless times, sometimes what can happen is that you wed your current spouse for the very first time.

The history of humankind is not as short as it is currently thought to be. It is much, much longer and naturally, people do not marry the same person every time. Our marriage partners change many times.

This being said, there is an extremely high likelihood that you will marry somebody with whom you have had some kind of relationship in the past. While it is difficult to put a figure to it, I would say that there is about a 99 percent chance that you have known each other in a previous life.

Even though you and your spouse may be married for the first time, in a past life you two may have been extremely close siblings; you may have made a promise to each other to be a couple in this lifetime because you really wanted to live together. Or, you may become a couple for the first time in this life with someone with whom you have had some kind of strong personal tie, even if the two of you were not related by blood in the past.

But in most cases or over 90 percent of cases, you would be coupled with someone whom you have married before sometime in your past lives.

Do not get too hung up on
The "red string of fate"

What if you marry somebody other than the person you promised? This can sometimes happen. There are times when you cannot choose the right person.

For example, during the Pacific War several decades ago, large numbers of men were killed and the result was that there were several times as many women as men.

Did all these women come down to earth prepared to be single all their lives? The answer is no. Although they had chosen the partner they wanted to marry, those men died in the war. This kind of thing happens.

If you are tossed about by such conditions in the society, sometimes you cannot meet the best partner as planned. What happens in such cases? In most cases, you will find somebody else with whom you have had some kind of relationship in the past and be attracted to one another.

When you and someone else are reborn into the same era, it is not with that person alone. It is quite common to be born with a group of people who lived around the same time as you in past lives.

With regard to the bond between a couple, while it is true to say that there is a best combination where you could say, "Mr. A and Miss B would be the best match," there are various levels of compatibility and there are also other partners in reserve. Normally, people have at least two or three options in reserve in case their first choice does not work out or the person intended as your partner has already married someone else.

While it is true that people promise to get married, they may get caught up in some kind of confusion in this world and, of their own free will, end up marrying someone they had not originally intended to.

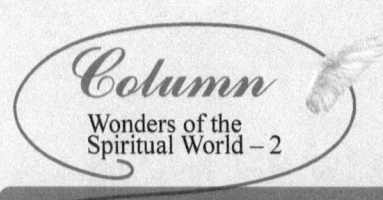

How Does the Process of Reincarnation Work?

In the spiritual messages of Princess Kozakura [see *Okawa Ryuho Reigen Zenshu, 26* (A Collection of Spiritual Messages by Ryuho Okawa, Vol. 26) (Tokyo: Happy Science, 2004)], she talks about the "pond of reincarnation."

When spirits want to be reborn into this world, they walk through the "forest of reincarnation" to go to the "pond of reincarnation" found on its outskirts. There is a cliff that is about ten feet high. When they look down from the cliff they can see the pond.

If they look at it carefully, they will notice that it has no bottom; instead, they can see through into this world. It will also show an image of where they will be born in this world. They are able to see the kind of place they will be born in, as well as the professions of their parents-to-be.

At this point some hesitate to dive into the pond because they cannot follow through with their decisions. Then their guardian spirits will come and encourage them, "You have finally made up your mind to be reborn, so you must do it. You have come this far, so you cannot turn back now. Be brave and try again." Being persuaded in this way for thirty minutes to an hour, they will finally make up their mind and say, "All right, I will go now," and plunge into the pond.

This is the worldview of Princess Kozakura, a female spirit who was born in Japan four or five hundred years ago. She has a worldview that states, "There is a place called the 'forest of reincarnation' where there is a shrine dedicated to a local Shinto deity and, after discussing the matter with this deity, spirits are given permission to jump into the 'pond of reincarnation' to be reborn." In the vast Spirit World, she now resides in the sixth-dimensional realm in the Japanese Shinto section. This kind of mechanism for rebirth is operating in her section.

There are also more rational methods of rebirth than diving into the pond of reincarnation. For instance, there is a modern facility for rebirth. This is a dome-shaped building inside which there is an aisle. Spirits walk up this aisle in the company of their guardian spirits and are sent off at the entrance of the dome, receiving good wishes for their new departure. They will enter the inner part of the dome, where other spirits preparing to be reborn are sitting on chairs and putting on something that resembles headphones.

There, they are shown something like a movie that teaches them how to prepare for rebirth. This lasts one or two hours, showing the entire lives of different people or the various mistakes others have made. They watch many of these films that are adjusted to their preferences.

For example, if a spirit presses the button to see a case of a person who was born in the same area as where he will be born in but who failed in life, the film of that person's life will be shown and the spirit will be able to learn how to avoid making the same mistakes. In this way, spirits prepare themselves for birth until eventually they fall into a kind of hypnosis and are reborn into this world. There is such a mechanism for rebirth.

In fact, the mechanism for rebirth differs according to the level of the realm where the spirit resides.

Gain Knowledge of This World and the Next and Lead A Happy Life

[Chapter 3]

You are Not Alone in Life

What is A Guardian Spirit?

One of the soul siblings takes
The role of a guardian spirit

A human being is essentially a body of energy and there is more to an individual than just the soul that inhabits the physical body. In the same way that starfish have numerous arms, the spiritual body is divided into a number of parts like the head, arms and legs. These parts are called "soul siblings."

When one of these inhabits a physical body and lives in this world, one of the remaining parts of the spiritual body – a part that is a hand, foot or brain – will take the role of a guardian spirit, remaining in the other world and continuing to send numerous messages about life's journey to the person living on earth.

A guardian spirit is not omniscient
But has a higher level of awareness
Than the person on earth

Those living in the other world are on a higher plane compared to those living on earth, so they are able to see more than those who live in this world. That is why they send various messages as warnings before people on earth stumble.

Of course, the level of consciousness of the guardian spirit does not differ greatly from that of the person on earth, so if the person here has not achieved a high degree of enlightenment, the messages sent from the Spirit World would not be of a high level, either.

Nevertheless, the guardian spirit is sure to possess a higher level of awareness than the person on earth. Therefore, it is important that you live in a way that enables you to receive messages from your own soul sibling who is acting daily as your guardian spirit. This is the first step toward a life of happiness.

The Mechanism of Soul Siblings And the Guardian Spirit

In principle, a soul is formed of a group of six soul siblings. The leader is called the "core spirit" while the other five are called "branch spirits."

branch spirit

branch spirit

core spirit

branch spirit

branch spirit

branch spirit

The soul that dwells in a physical body and lives on earth

Guardian Spirit

The six spirits are born into this world in turns and one of the five remaining in the heavenly world takes the role of the guardian spirit.

Why Do I Continue to Experience Unhappiness Despite Having A Guardian Spirit?

Your guardian spirit watches over you every day

When I talk about the other world and say, "Everyone has an own guardian spirit who watches over him all the time," then those who lack faith will quickly snap back by saying, "If I have a guardian spirit, why am I so unhappy?" "Why did I fail in running a company?" "Why can't I make money?" "Why did members of my family get sick and die? It can't be true."

There are people who say, "If my guardian spirit does exist, it should surely protect me. But actually it doesn't, so I cannot believe in it." These people tend to choose unhappiness. They are the type of people who think the worst about everything.

I have been observing for a long time and I can tell you that your guardian spirit really does watch over your way of life every day, experiencing your joys and sorrows with you.

The guardian spirit takes the role of A driving instructor while the person On earth actually takes the wheel

In principle, the person living on earth in physical form is undergoing soul training for this lifetime, so it is the person on earth who actually has the responsibility for his own life.

If the person on earth were completely controlled by the guardian spirit like a puppet like some kind of Pinocchio, then there would be no point to the soul training a person undertakes in this world. It would be meaningless. For this reason, the guardian spirit is not allowed to be totally in control. This is something of a dilemma.

The guardian spirit is always with you, much like a back-seat driver, and says, "You should not go that way. Go this way instead." While it can offer advice in this way, it is not allowed to actually take the wheel and drive in place of you.

This relationship is similar to the one between you and your instructor at a driving school. Your guardian spirit is like a driving instructor sitting beside you. When he sees danger approaching, he will step on the brakes. But he cannot actually take hold of the steering wheel and drive in your place, because that would not teach you anything. This is how the guardian spirit works.

Since the training ground in this world is different from that of the other world, this is an unchangeable principle. We have no choice but to accept it. Nevertheless, I would like you to believe that when danger approaches, there is always somebody [your guardian spirit] who is willing to provide you with a warning and guide you in a better direction.

What Should I Do to Get Guidance From My Guardian Spirit?

The guardian spirit has its own life In the other world

People on earth are prone to arrogance and they tend to think, "If I have a guardian spirit, then it is sure to come and save me when I am in danger" or "A guiding spirit embodies love and mercy, so it is sure to come and drive away any evil spirit whenever needed."

However, according to the various experiences I have had in the last 30 years or so, the guardian and guiding spirits have their own work to do in the other world and they come to help you only at important turning points in your life.

You need to know that they have their own lives to lead in the other world. For example, when you are at the office, tapping the keys on your calculator every day, your guardian spirit is not there pressing the keys with you. Your guiding spirit is not watching over you all day long, either.

Guardian and guiding spirits are like parents watching a small child playing in a park; they oversee your general situation but do not bother with the details or tell you when to turn left and right. The details are basically left to the discretion of the person on earth.

Your prayers will definitely reach Your guardian spirit

When you think, "I need the protection of my guardian and guiding spirit now," you can ask for their assistance in a clear fashion. Let's say that a child playing in a sandbox in a park calls out for his mother or father. His parent will quickly go to the child to see what he wants. In the same way, when the guardian and guiding spirits notice that you are in need of their assistance, they will come to you straight away.

Pray to your guardian and guiding spirits, properly and clearly, for example, "I need you to protect me from evil spirits now," "I want your assistance to purify this spiritual environment, so that I can practice self-reflection," or "I am now going to offer a ritual prayer.

Please guide me, so that I do not pray for the wrong purpose. Please protect me, so that evil spirits will not come and tempt me with desires." If you are a member of Happy Science, you can use "Prayer to Guardian and Guiding Spirits*."

The prayer you have said in your mind will be transmitted almost instantly to the other world. It only takes about thirty seconds to one minute to recite "Prayer to Guardian and Guiding Spirits" and while you are reciting it, your guardian and guiding spirits come close to you. Therefore, as a basic way to practice self-reflection or prayer, it is advisable to start by reciting "Prayer to Guardian and Guiding Spirits."

You can recite this prayer every day. By doing so, the feeling of oneness with your guardian and guiding spirits will be strengthened even more. But when you pray to your guardian and guiding spirits, you must be willing to examine yourself with a humble attitude.

---

* The prayer is included in *Prayers Book I*, which people who pledge devotion to the Three Treasures receive. The prayer is also included in the blue prayer book that people receive upon joining Happy Science as a member.

Gain Knowledge of This World and the Next and Lead A Happy Life

[Chapter 4]

You Can Become an Angel Too

Do Angels Really Exist?

Angels actually exist

These days, most people have difficulty believing that angels and devils exist outside fairy tales and dismiss the notion with a laugh.

Christianity is based on "the Father, the Son and the Holy Spirit." Although many Christians may seem like they understand God the Father and the Son, they have difficulty understanding the Holy Spirit.

Even devout Christians who accept the existence of the angels described in the Bible can be uncomfortable believing in them as actual entities. However, angels really do exist, as do devils, which is why stories about them can be found throughout history in both the East and the West and in advanced as well as developing countries.

There are hundreds of millions of angels whose job Is to save people who have just left this world

The word "angels" refers to the high spirits. Those known as angels come from the upper part of the sixth dimension and above. These are the divinities that we have recognized throughout history as saints and gods when they took on human form. The high spirits that reside in the seventh and eighth dimensions, known as bodhisattvas and tathagatas respectively, are also angels.

At their initial level of training, angels become responsible for people who have just departed from the three-dimensional world. At this stage, angels are engaged in the practical tasks of saving souls. They act as guides for people who have just left their bodies, looking after them and educating them. These angels number in the hundreds of millions and change their appearance according to the ideology, beliefs and religion of the deceased. Angels from the Christian spirit group generally look after and guide Christians, bodhisattvas from the Buddhist spirit group provide guidance to Buddhists, and so on. These angels appear in whatever form makes it easy for the recently deceased to accept them.

Angels are sometimes born into this world

Angels not only exist in the other world but also live in this one. Most angels reincarnate on earth repeatedly, although the frequency of their reincarnation varies widely, from every few hundred years to every thousand years. They are born here for the purpose of training their souls and purifying the world but they also come down to remind themselves what it is like to live as human beings. If they remain in the other world for too long, it becomes difficult for them to understand how people on earth think or feel. So in order to become better teachers of souls, angels need to come down periodically and take on human form.

An added advantage of being born on earth in this way is that by understanding human sensibilities, they are able to preach God's Truths to a wide variety of people while still giving each person the specific teachings they need. This allows them to lead as many people as possible to salvation.

Mini Column 3

The Love of Angels

You may not be aware of the fact that angels are giving guidance in churches or consoling people in places where wars are being fought. You probably do not know that they are working upon people to bring peace to the world, either.

The people of this world are unable to see their activities. Their activities are indeed a transparent love.

Despite this, they never cease to carry out their activities. Even though people in this world cannot understand their activities nor recognize their presence, or even if people deny their existence saying, "Angels do not exist. The other world does not exist. Spirits do not exist," angels never stop helping the people on earth.

Who Were Some of the Angels [Bodhisattvas and Tathagatas] Who Descended to This World?

The World of Bodhisattvas of the seventh dimension — Religious leaders and other leaders who deal With problems of the mind

In the World of Bodhisattvas of the seventh dimension, there are many who, while alive in this world, devoted their lives to spreading the knowledge of Buddha's Truth or who established great projects that helped people without their even realizing it.

Religious leaders are the most common type in the World of Bodhisattvas of the seventh dimension, accounting for 70 or 80 percent of the total population. Mostly, people and leaders who offered guidance on problems of the mind while they were alive on earth come to this realm after death.

Of course, not everybody in this realm is a religious leader. Many of the leaders at the time of the Meiji Restoration in 19th century Japan, such as Kaishu

Katsu, Ryoma Sakamoto and Shoin Yoshida, became bodhisattvas after death and, even today, they are active in the World of Bodhisattvas. Also, many of the leaders of different countries who had a respectable heart come to this World of Bodhisattvas after death.

The World of Tathagatas of the eighth dimension — Those who create the highpoint of an era With their own philosophy

The world of the eighth dimension, above the World of Bodhisattvas, is the place where tathagatas reside. Currently there are fewer than 500 tathagatas in this realm. Tathagatas are, of course, those who have advanced from the bodhisattva state. Those who have the ability to found a religious sect or create the highpoint of an era are referred to as tathagatas.

To give some examples of tathagatas who have been active in Japanese history, there were Prince Shotoku [574-622] and the Buddhist monk Kukai [774-835]. The original spiritual level of the Buddhist monk Nichiren [1222-1282] is also that of tathagata, though he is currently working in the Brahma Realm on the border between the World of Bodhisattvas and the World of Tathagatas. In this Brahma Realm are also the philosopher Yukichi Fukuzawa [1835-1901] and the religious leader Masaharu Taniguchi [1893-1985]. More recently, the philosopher Kanzo Uchimura [1861-1930] and the religious leader Onisaburo Deguchi [1871-1948] were also Tathagatas.

Tathagatas are those who can establish and leave behind a fundamental philosophy or who become the pillar of a religion. They are people who can create civilizations and cultures with their own philosophies. People with such original thoughts are tathagatas.

The Cosmic World of the ninth dimension — Buddha, Christ, Confucius and other saviors

Above the World of Tathagatas of the eighth dimension is the Cosmic World of the ninth dimension where Messiahs reside.

The ninth dimension is where you can find the Great Guiding Spirits of Light such as Shakyamuni Buddha, Jesus Christ, Confucius, Manu, Maitreya, Koot Hoomi [Newton], Zoroaster, Zeus, Moses and Enlil. Shakyamuni Buddha is a part of the huge life form called El Cantare, the central being among the spirits of the ninth dimension and the highest leader of the terrestrial spirit group.

For further information on this, please refer to my books, *The Golden Laws* [New York: Lantern Books, 2011] and *The Nine Dimensions* [New York: IRH Press, 2012]. These Great Guiding Spirits of Light also descend to earth every few thousand years to preach the Laws.

Can I Become An Angel Too?

Everybody has the potential to become an angel

Angels of Light are what are referred to in Buddhism as tathagatas and bodhisattvas. In a nutshell, they can be described as people who display outstanding leadership in working to create utopia. Those who have won recognition for their work in previous incarnations become tathagatas and bodhisattvas. Therefore, all of you have the potential to become tathagatas or bodhisattvas in the future.

How to become an angel

In order to become an angel, you have to build up a record of leadership in your efforts to create utopia. However, this is no easy matter; if your ability to be a leader declines in the course of your reincarnations, you could lose your status as an Angel of Light. The converse is also true; if your leadership abilities improve, your light can increase even further.

This is due to the fact that the Spirit World is governed by clear rules, one of which states that if you work hard, your light will increase but if you get lazy, it will decrease. The opportunities to advance are offered equally and the results of effort are rewarded fairly. This is a basic rule. Opportunities are always offered equally. Everybody can advance, regardless of their starting point. And the results are always rewarded fairly.

The fact that there is such a clear rule is something to be extremely thankful for. It is because such a clear rule exists that, for hundreds of millions of years, humans have been able to continue undergoing soul training and are able to see the worth of working toward this.

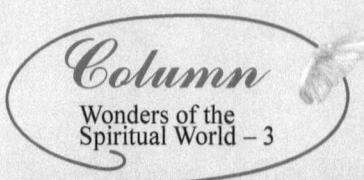

A Conversation with Mother Teresa In the Spirit World

Mother Teresa, known as Blessed Teresa of Calcutta, died in Calcutta [present-day Kolkata] in the autumn of 1997. After her death, I decided to contact her.

Directly contacting a person whom you did not know personally soon after his death can give rise to various problems, so usually this is done through an intermediary. Whenever I want to do this, I get in touch with a spirit I have known for a long time and ask it to serve as the intermediary given that there is no problem in making contact.

Although Christians may find this hard to believe, the spirit I contacted at the time was my very old friend, Jesus Christ. When I told him that I wished to contact Mother Teresa, he arranged for us to talk briefly.

I used the word "talk" but if the one I contact is an angel [high spirit], it is possible for us to go beyond words and communicate directly through telepathy. But in a case where the meeting occurs soon after the person's death, this can be a little difficult. So when I talked to Mother Teresa, we communicated in English through our thoughts. Her English had great originality; she spoke in short phrases.

When I asked her about her feelings, she replied, "My work is in the slums. I know that I died and returned to the Spirit World but I wish to go back to the slums and carry on my work of salvation."

She lived until the age of 87, dedicating her life to religion, so she did not yearn over her worldly life. Still, she retained some attachment to her work in the slums. What I said to her was as follows: "Being too attached to the poor or slum-dwellers is not necessarily in accordance with God's Will. The heavenly world is a very rich and beautiful place; those who reside there are all broad-minded and enjoy freedom. Even if you are thinking of something good, if you allow your heart to remain bound to one thing, you will find yourself unable to harmonize with the relaxing freedom of the heavenly world.

"While you were on earth, you saved the poor and fulfilled the work of a bodhisattva. But now that you returned to the Spirit World, you need to learn its rules and ways and study more about what the heavenly world is like." This is how I advised her.

When I talked to her in this way, she was still near the entrance of the fourth dimension because it was soon after she passed away. While in the fourth dimension, she will have to learn about the other world and cast off her old self. Once she has studied there for a certain length of time, she will move on to the fifth dimension where she will continue her studies before graduating to the sixth. Eventually, she will have to move on to the World of Bodhisattvas of the seventh dimension, her original home. In her case, this will take about two or three years from the time of her death. During this time, she must learn about the Spirit World.

How to Protect Yourself Against Negative Spiritual Influences

[Chapter 1]

Memorial Services That Can Truly Save The Spirits in the Other World

Are My Series of Misfortunes Caused By My Ancestors Being Lost?

The reason for your unhappiness does not lie In the lost spirits of your ancestors

There is a line of thinking that says, "Your current unhappiness is due to the fact that your ancestors have not been saved." Using this logic, many religious groups say, "You are unhappy now because an ancestor some generations back is yet to be saved" or "The source of your unhappiness lies not in you but in your ancestors."

Of course, I do not intend to say flatly that this is wrong. Sometimes in reality it actually is true that the spirits of a person's parents, grandparents or ancestors are lost and come to the living in search of help. It is true that unhappiness sometimes arises due to this kind of spiritual disturbance.

Fundamentally speaking, however, the real cause lies in the mind of the person living on earth. That is what will determine a person's happiness or unhappiness. Even if a person has an ancestor whose spirit is still lost, it is the way that the person here on earth leads his life that will decide whether he will fall to Hell. This has nothing to do with his ancestor's spirit.

There is the Law of Same Wavelengths' Attraction;* it is because a person is leading a hellish lifestyle that he becomes possessed by the lost spirits of his ancestors, as a result of this law. They share the same suffering, as the proverb says, "fellow sufferers pity each other." In other words, the person is not unhappy because he is possessed; rather, it is because he retains feelings of unhappiness that he invites his lost ancestors to come and possess him.

While it is certainly very important to hold memorial services for your ancestors, the principle of self-responsibility exists. First, you must start with yourself – before you hope to save the dead, you have to save the living. That is to say, unless you, yourself, save your own mind, nobody else is going to save it for you. Once you give out a bright and happy light, you will be able to save your ancestors as well.

On the other hand, if you are the kind of person who is likely to fall straight to Hell, as long as you blame your misfortunes on your family or your ancestors, you will never be able to achieve happiness. Do not

---

* A law that states, "similar wavelengths or states of mind attract one another." For more details, refer to *The Mystical Laws* [Tokyo: Happy Science, 2012], Chapter Two.

misunderstand this point. Please know that in principle, you are the one who must take responsibility for your own happiness or unhappiness.

This is a good guideline for checking to see if a religious group is misguided or not. If it puts the blame on other things outside the self, it is generally wrong. Self-responsibility is the basic rule.

What is the Proper Way to Conduct Memorial Services for Ancestors?

The power of enlightenment is necessary in Conducting memorial services for ancestors

In order to hold memorial services for ancestors, the premise is that those who conduct the services must be undergoing spiritual training. First you need to study Buddha's Truth, read books on the Truth, participate in different kinds of seminars at Happy Science, deepen your knowledge of the Truth and train yourself so that you can feel the light of Buddha. As a result of all these efforts, you will be able to transmit some of that light to your ancestors.

It will be impossible for you to shine a light out to the sea in darkness unless you become a lighthouse yourself. When a ship is lost in the night, unable to find its course, if there is no light shining from the lighthouse, no matter how much you want to save the ship, you cannot be of help. Rather than desperately saying that you want to save it when you, yourself, are groping in the dark, you must first give out light, otherwise you cannot guide others.

In order for the people in this world to generate light, they need to study Buddha's Truth and undergo spiritual training. Not doing these but just conducting memorial services every day in an effort to save someone is questionable. Rather, you need to practice spiritual disciplines and increase the level of your enlightenment.

It is through the power of enlightenment that your ancestors can be saved. This is the starting point of memorial services.

Basically, entrust the salvation of Spiritual beings to high spirits

There are certain dangers involved in holding memorial services for ancestors, so I do not recommend that people conduct these too frequently at their home. That is why, at Happy Science, we hold Head Temple's Great Ceremony for Memorial Service for Ancestors, Perpetual Memorial Service and other services at Head Temple Shoshinkan.* Memorial services are also held once or twice a year at our branches throughout the world. It is much safer when there is a priest. You will

---

* Shoshinkan is a temple of Happy Science, a sacred place where prayers, religious training and worship take place.

also be protected by the light of other participants. So it is better for you to pray for the well-being of your ancestors on these occasions.

Furthermore, at our memorial service ceremonies, the guardian and guiding spirits of the participants, as well as the supporting spirits of Happy Science, will also be present and these spirits will discover the spirits possessing the homes of their descendants and causing trouble. The possessing spirits will feel ashamed at being told, "What are you doing here? It seems you have been causing these people trouble all these years," much like children being scolded by their teachers.

In fact, even in a case where descendants cannot save their ancestors with their own power alone, by taking part in Happy Science's memorial services, the high spirits will do that; they will reprimand the spirits who are doing wrong. Spirits are the most knowledgeable when it comes to the other world, so it is best to leave the correction of errors of spirits up to the high spirits. This is the quickest way.

Attending Happy Science events will provide you with the opportunity to create a new relationship with the high spirits in this way. So when it comes to memorial services for ancestors it is recommended that you take part in one of the Happy Science ceremonies.

Of course, it is not a bad thing for your family to gather to conduct memorial services several times a year, for instance, on the anniversary of a relative's death. However, do not do this too often. It is more important to undertake spiritual training diligently yourself than to pray for your ancestors every morning, afternoon and night, or before you go to bed.

Focus your efforts on increasing the level of your enlightenment by reciting Happy Science's fundamental sutra, *Buddha's Teaching: The Dharma of the Right Mind*,* or by reading and studying books on Buddha's Truth. Conduct memorial services in places where a priest is present, if possible. This has the lowest risk and is the most effective way.

---

* The fundamental sutra book will be given exclusively to Happy Science devotees who pledge devotion to the Three Treasures of Buddha, Dharma and Sangha.

Do I Need to Conduct Memorial Services for My Dead Pets?

Animals will soon be reborn, so it is pointless
To hold memorial services for
A long period of time

In most cases, a pet will be reborn soon after death and will only remain in the other world for about 10 years at the longest. Generally, most animals will return to this world in about one year; they only stay in the other world for a short while.

There is, of course, nothing wrong with conducting memorial services for dead pets, but it is meaningless to continue doing so for very long. Rather, if you do services for them for a long period of time, they would take it to mean that they have to remain in the place where you are offering your prayers and would stay there indefinitely. This can hinder their next reincarnation.

The soul of the rabbit that my family used to keep reincarnated about one month after it died. Rabbit souls form a collective group in the Spirit World and are reborn from there. They enter the womb of the mother rabbit and are reborn in quick succession.

Considering this, continuing to conduct memorial services for dead pets for a long time is rather questionable.

Part 3

How to Protect Yourself Against Negative Spiritual Influences

[Chapter 2]

Do Evil Spirits Truly Exist?

What are Evil Spirits?

Evil spirits are those who have misused Their free will

People who believe in the existence of the Spirit World may wonder about the existence of ghosts. Although people have heard of ghosts in fairy tales or horror stories, they do not imagine spirits having anything to do with their reality. In the unseen world, however, evil spirits are certainly active and are trying to influence us.

So what are these spirits? The best way to describe them is as spirits who are responsive to the negative energy emitted by human beings,* that is to say, the energy of people's negative thoughts. People who constantly have negative thoughts while they are alive on earth go to the hellish realm after they die and live there as stray spirits.

---

* Concrete examples of negative energy are jealousy, anger, complaints, the mental attitude of not knowing how to be content, grumbling, pessimistic thoughts, laziness, hatred, etc. For more information, refer to *The Laws of the Sun*, Chapter Three.

In other words, stray spirits were not originally created at the beginning of time; they are those who strayed from the right path in the process of living. Anyone could become a stray spirit.

As human beings, we have been granted the freedom to hold any thought we want in our minds and by exercising this freedom, we are able to change our very being. Through full use of this freedom of thought, people are able to turn themselves into either beings of good or beings of evil. Stray spirits are those who failed to use this freedom correctly.

What are Demons? How are They Different from Evil Spirits?

A demon has greater influence, greater leadership Qualities and are more cunning than evil spirits

Ordinary people can become evil spirits if they harbor evil thoughts or do evil deeds. People do not necessarily have to commit crimes in order to become evil spirits. They can become evil spirits if they live their lives with bad or negative thoughts.

Characteristics of an evil spirit include: always thinking of doing evil, fighting with people, trying to deceive or hurt others, always feeling angry, harming people without feeling guilt and living with destructive thoughts or emotions. Evil spirits are souls that were unable to return to Heaven and went to a place called Hell, where they will continue to suffer and rage because they caused suffering to those all around them.

On the other hand, a demon has a bit more influence or leadership and is more cunning than a typical evil spirit.

What kind of people become Demons after death?

Demons mostly come from those who have been in leadership positions. For example, misguided political leaders or dictators can easily become devils. Pol Pot [1928-1998], the Cambodian dictator who was responsible for the deaths of two million of his people, is undoubtedly a demon. Hitler [1889-1945] and Stalin [1878-1953] are as well. Those with political power whose regimes led to many murders have become demons after they died.

There are leaders who kill large numbers of people because they truly enjoy cruelty and brutality and wish to enforce their power and control over others through fear. These people will most likely become demons.

Moreover, while they may not be related to politics or the military, thinkers who misguide or brainwash many people are also likely to become demons. Among those who were in influential positions, those who ultimately have done great evil are likely to become demons.

There are also differences in the power of demons. In modern times, there are people in the media or journalism who have great influence in this world. Those in this industry who work for the sake of fulfilling their own desires or greed, rather than for the sake of society and justice, become small demons. There are many people who become small devils and have about five or six minions.

There are also thinkers and authors who become demons through presenting their thinking in books. There are many novelists who are writing evil literature and have brainwashed large numbers of people. Hellish literature is quite popular in this world and there are some famous writers who become demons. Those whose work has resulted in the corruption and negligence of others have the disposition to become demons. There are also bureaucrats who became demons because they lacked a compassionate heart and lived only to gain power.

Religious leaders influence a great number of people, so a leader of a misguided religion will become a demon with very little hope of returning to Heaven. Not only did they disseminate wrong teachings but they also misled many people. They misled people not only in this world but have dragged them into Hell and created a base camp of the followers of their religion. These are the very actions of demons and devils. Misguiding people's hearts is a great sin.

What is Spiritual Possession?

Evil spirits possess people,
Drawn to their clouded minds

Basically, humans rely on their superficial consciousness to live, but in the course of their lives they create various kinds of "clouds" over their minds. Most of these clouds are created by disharmonious phenomena sprung from thoughts or actions which go against the Will of Buddha.

When you harbor thoughts that are against Buddha's Will or Buddha's Desires, or act in a way that is not in accordance with His Will, a kind of "smog" gradually builds up around your mind. In other words, shadows will appear over your mind. Then, your superficial consciousness, which is only a small portion of your whole mind, becomes covered in dust and dirt, gradually cutting off contact with your subconscious.

If your mind is pure, the original nature of your soul will surface and your tendencies and Buddha-nature* will be apparent. However, sometimes clouds can form around your superficial consciousness. In terms of Buddha's Truth, this part of the mind is not exactly the superficial consciousness but an area called the "Thought Tape."

The Thought Tape lies between the superficial consciousness and the subconscious. As clouds form over this Thought Tape, the superficial consciousness and the subconscious will gradually be separated from each other and the Light of Buddha will no longer reach the person's mind.

When this happens, a certain sort of beings gradually come closer to the shadow of that darkened mind. These are the beings known as "evil spirits." Evil spirits try desperately to possess people on earth in order to escape from the agony of Hell. In this way, people on earth come under the control of evil spirits.

However, it is not the evil spirits who are completely at fault; it is the person on earth who has taken the actions that caused this to happen. It is not the sun's fault that its light gets cut off by the clouds. In the same way, it is not Buddha's fault that His Light† does not shine onto a person's mind. The responsibility lies with

---

* Buddha-nature refers to the same attributes as Buddha, such as love, mercy and the aspiration to improve. Human beings are children of Buddha and everyone is endowed with Buddha-nature.

† Buddha's light is the energy of Buddha filling the great universe. All human souls live while absorbing and releasing Buddha's Light.

the person who created the clouds of thought energy that block the light. These clouds create shadows and in turn produce darkness. Then, according to the law of "like attracts like," evil spirits are drawn to this darkness.

Evil spirits will leave if you remove The clouds from your mind

People on earth might go to exorcists to have evil spirits removed, hang holy charms on their walls to keep evil spirits at bay or carry holy amulets to protect themselves. However, what scares evil spirits the most is somebody who lives with the mind of Buddha as his own.

When an exorcist has spiritual, supernatural or psychic powers, he can certainly expel the evil spirits with the light of exorcism, but it only has a temporary effect. Once the person who has been exorcised leaves that place, the effect will soon wane and evil spirits will again be drawn to the same clouded areas of the mind.

Therefore, no matter how many times the person may drive out evil spirits, the spirits will soon return. It is exactly the same as trying to shoo away a fly - no matter how hard you shoo it away, it will come back again. That is because there is something there that attracts it. That is the mechanism of spiritual possession.

In short, it is nothing but your own mind that

attracts evil spirits. The clouds over your mind are the root of the problem. Therefore, by removing the clouds from your mind, evil spirits will have no choice but to leave. This is the truth I want to teach here.

The Structure of the Mind and The Mechanism of Spiritual Possession

The Thought Tape:
This lies between the superficial consciousness and the subconscious and records all the thoughts and deeds in your lifetime.

The superficial consciousness

The subconscious

Buddha-nature

The clouds in the thought tape

Influence of evil spirits [spiritual possession]:

When you think or act in a way that goes against Buddha's Will, clouds will form over the Thought Tape. Evil spirits then begin to possess this portion of the mind. The clouds over the mind can be removed by practicing self-reflection.

How Can We Defeat Evil Spirits and Demons?

Do not negotiate with demons, Just drive them away

Demons have been in the other world for one, two or even three thousand years, so it is nearly impossible for them to go to Heaven through persuasion. Some people will say strange things when they are possessed and it is useless to persuade the possessing demon to leave the person. Demons will try very hard to deceive and trick people. A demon may come crying and begging to you saying, "Please help me," "I have changed my ways" or "Please take me in as a disciple," but these are all lies, so do not believe them. A demon will think nothing of shedding tears.

Do not negotiate with demons. Simply exorcise them; drive them away with a strong will to stop and prevent further spreading of evil.

A spirit who has just died and is lost can be persuaded to return to Heaven, but the same cannot be done to demons. Demons have sinned that much. Against demons, it is important that you do not allow them to commit further sins.

If you increase the power of light and fight As a team, you can overcome demons

Since demons, themselves, will not disappear right away, I focus on increasing the domain of light and closing them in. My strategy is to create forts or bases of light all over the world, enclosing the demons and gradually reducing their habitat. This is a long battle. There are so many demons. We will not be able to win just by fighting against them; we need to increase the power of Happy Science itself.

However, true to character, demons are not able to cooperate with each other. We should be glad about this. We would be in trouble if a large number of devils cooperated with each other and joined forces as one, but they fight on an individual basis. I am very glad about this.

We would be in a grave situation if all the demons in Hell, which would be hundreds or thousands or some large number, got together and attacked us as one. But demons cannot work together and will fight amongst themselves, so they will always attack individually.

Demons always work individually and act at will because they cannot cooperate and work together.

To fight against demons, it is important to create a power of light in which we form a united front and work together, hand in hand. If demons, too, could form a common front to fight together, maybe they would start to think as a team and learn to love one another.

Usually, a demon matching an individual's concerns or situation at the time will come near that person. But because demons attack individually and not as an organized unit, if we fight as an organization, we can win.

The most effective method of exorcism is to do it in a place that has an established spiritual vibration, like a Happy Science local branch or temple, and to have it conducted by a professional priest who has accumulated much spiritual training. If an ordinary member performs it, there is a chance he may be defeated due to insufficient spiritual power. If possible, it is better to have it conducted by a professional disciple in a place with an established spiritual vibration, as opposed to doing it yourself.

Mini Column 4

The Sacred Rite To Exorcise Demons

In Happy Science, as a sacred rite to exorcise demons, members are given "El Cantare Fight" and it is being practiced all over the world.

Spiritual power will come from the El Cantare consciousness if the people who perform El Cantare Fight have faith and know that they are receiving the Light of El Cantare. If you understand that you are repelling evil with the Light of El Cantare, demons will have to face El Cantare. Therefore, you must understand that you are fighting evil together as an organization, united with the heavenly world.

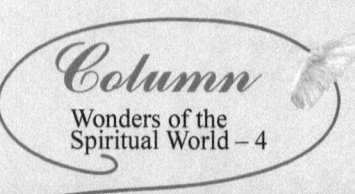

Column

Wonders of the
Spiritual World – 4

The Network in the Depths of Our Minds That Connects All Existence

In 12th - 13th century Japan, there was a distinguished priest belonging to the Hua-yen sect of Buddhism with the name, Myoe [1173-1232]. Apparently, he was a psychic. If you study the literature on his life, you will come across the following story:

One night he was sitting in meditation by the fireplace of the temple, looking as if he were fast asleep when suddenly he spoke to one of his disciples. "Poor thing. It might be too late now, but there is a sparrow, in a nest under the eaves of the bathroom, about to be eaten by a snake. Hurry, take a light and drive the snake away." The disciple did not really believe him but, taking a lantern, went to the back of the house and found that just as his master had said, there was a snake poised to eat a sparrow. Despite the darkness, Myoe had been able to see what was happening in another place.

This is possible for those who possess psychic abilities; they can actually see what is happening somewhere distant. This kind of phenomenon is common. Even people like him are unable to find out things when they are immersed in the rough vibrations of this world, however, when they are in a state of meditation, they can see these things very clearly.

When you enter into deep meditation, you will connect to different worlds and be able to see all kinds of things. You will be able to understand the workings of the minds of animals as well as the thoughts and feelings of plants. As you further deepen your meditative state, your consciousness will reach this far. And you will come to know the thinking or feelings of someone with whom you have some tie, no matter how far away that person may be. Through that connection, you will naturally be able to feel what the other person is actually thinking right now.

In my case, for example, if I want to know what the president of a country is thinking at any particular time, I am able to do so within the range allowed by Heaven. In the same way that it is possible to access a computer and retrieve information, I can understand what the target person is thinking. If I take too much interest, I could even find myself in trouble from all the crucial information coming in.

In this way, by going deep within yourself, you can find a road that leads to an infinite universe. And from this infinite universe, it connects to each and every person. This ultimately means that everything that has been granted life on this earth, including non-human existence, retains traces as created beings. Be they humans, animals or plants, all bear the traces of creation.

What are the traces of creation? They are in the power that allows a living being to exist. This power can be referred to as "Buddha-nature." It manifests itself as the laws of the mind. All living beings exist within and live in accordance with the laws of the mind; this is the trace as created beings.

A Correct Understanding of Buddha and God

[Chapter 1]

Recognize the Great Love of Buddha and God

Does God Really Exist?
Is There Any Proof?

God as the Prime Cause

Since ancient times, people have done huge amounts of research and inquiry into the nature of God. For instance, there were some who discussed God as the "Prime Cause." They stated:

"All things have a cause. You are living today because you had parents. They are the cause of your existence. Your parents also existed because they had parents, as well as their parents before them. In this way, without exception, everything has a precursor. For every effect there is a cause. This being so, if things were to be traced back indefinitely, we would ultimately end up back at the Prime Cause. This Prime Cause is indeed God." There were philosophers and theologians who proved God's existence in this way.

Everything in this world bears traces As created beings

Considering that every effect has a cause, it is logical, even from common sense, to assume that there was a being that created this world.

Nowadays it is popular to believe that this world came into being by chance but, seen from a longer-term or broader perspective, I have to say that this thinking makes no sense at all.

Is it likely that humans just appeared by chance? Is it really possible that humans evolved randomly from amoeba?

Humans are like skyscrapers, so to speak. They are like 40- or 50-story buildings: planned, designed, and constructed by someone. Nevertheless, today's mainstream scholars who support the theory of evolution claim that humans came into being with their current physical body and spirit through a succession of accidental events.

This is the same as saying that some sand, gravel, blocks and reinforcing bars were left lying around on the ground when, coincidentally, a wind blew, rain fell and concrete mixed itself. Then by coincidence something like an earthquake occurred that caused the bars to form a cage and, before you knew it, a skyscraper was built.

However, the more we know about the intricate structure of human beings, the clearer it becomes that we are not the result of any accidental assembly of materials. Human beings actually are created with a purpose.

The truth is that everything in this world bears traces as created beings. This is true of all living beings, including minerals. By the same token, non-living objects like buildings have an original cause — the people who constructed them. This being so, it is only natural to assume that God exists as the Prime Cause.

If God Exists, Why is There Evil In the World?

Does the absolute nature of God really contradict The existence of evil?

Since ancient times, religious leaders and philosophers have debated the existence of good and evil. They have been arguing, "If God is an absolute being and there is only good in Him, then evil should not exist; evil spirits and demons should not exist. If these beings do exist, would it mean that God also embodies the same attributes and nature as them? Or, if He doesn't, then it would mean that there is a world where God's rule does not cover; therefore, we cannot say that God governs the entire universe. This would then mean that other powers exist and that God is not the one and only, the absolute." This has been the subject of such controversy and when it comes to good and evil, people have not been able to reach any conclusion since ancient times.

On the island of Bali in Indonesia, there is a folk dance known as the Barong dance. The dance portrays

Barong, the leader of the good spirits and an ethnic god, and Rangda, the embodiment of evil and a demon incarnate. The power of the good or true god, Barong, and the evil god or devil, Rangda, are equal. Neither of them can get the upper hand, so the battle of good against evil continues indefinitely.

This philosophy is also a theme described in the ancient Middle-Eastern religion known as Zoroastrianism: the battle between good and evil or, to be more specific, the battle between the Angel of Light, the guiding spirit Ahura Mazda, and the evil god.

But is it really true that there are actually a good god and an evil god with equal power and that there is no winner to this battle?

Evil can be guided to goodness over time And by forgiveness

Indeed, if we look at human history, it seems as if good and evil have always existed and the battle between them continues without any conclusive result ever being reached. However, speaking from the true world of Buddha, there is a vast and monistic good that transcends the duality of good and evil; what appear to be good and evil to humans on earth are simply attributes that accompany freedom. These attributes appear differently in the eyes of humans.

Freedom, by its very nature, is limitless. That is what makes freedom what it is. By not having limits, freedom can bring about either a conflict or prosperity. In fact, if you look at the aspect of prosperity, freedom appears to be good, whereas if you take the aspect of conflict or strife, freedom appears to be evil. It is generally expected that this evil aspect is forgiven and transformed into good through the process of self-reflection, remorse or repentance.

The fact that this expectation is the premise for the existence of evil means that, if we look at this over a certain period of time, the monism of good can hold true. The monism of good states, "Looking at the decades of a lifetime, good and evil that can be clearly distinguished certainly exist. However, over the course of a longer span of time, all that appears to be evil will be instructed and led to good."

What seems to be an almost infinite period of time to a human is just a moment in Buddha's eyes. If we look at the world from this perspective, we can say that there is only good in the world that unfolds before our eyes.

Some people may feel that the existences of evil and evil deeds are unforgivable and wonder whether there is no Buddha or God in this world. They may question whether the powers of Buddha, God or bodhisattvas are no greater than that of demons. But to these people I would like to say, "Though something may appear evil at a certain point in time, know that over time, there is the religious act of forgiveness. And through forgiveness, everything can be taken as a process undergoing transformation into good."

If God Exists,
Why Does He Not Destroy Hell?

In a sense, Hell is a hospital

Hell is, in a sense, a place for punishment but in another sense, it is a hospital. The spirits in Hell are just like people who are sick. Therefore, the idea of destroying Hell is the same as the idea of eliminating the sick. If you drop a bomb on a hospital and totally destroy it, will that get rid of all sick people? Perhaps that idea is like saying, "Since the sick are abnormal, they should not be allowed to remain on earth."

There are no sick people to begin with. They were originally healthy people who, by not taking care of themselves or for some other reason, have become sick. However, even though they are sick now, they will eventually recover and become well again. Their true state is that of a healthy person. This is how Buddha thinks.

You, yourself, may get sick one day, too. If you do, you would not want to be exterminated. You were originally healthy, so you do not want people to say, "You have to go to a hospital but the patients in a hospital are of no use, so you should be killed" just because you got sick. Therefore, although Hell is a form of punishment, in a sense, it also functions like a hospital. So you should look at Hell in a more tolerant way.

It is possible that you could also end up in Hell. Ask yourself if you would really want your soul to be destroyed if that were to happen. Surely, you would rather choose to practice self-reflection and continue to live, even if it took you 500 years to reflect on yourself.

So please think of the spirits in Hell as people who are sick. They are not in their true form at the moment. They have become ill due to insufficient exercise, overeating or working too hard. Do you really think that this is sufficient reason to eliminate them or to say they really should not be allowed to exist? If you think deeply about this, you will come to understand that Buddha is so merciful that He has been waiting for quite a long time for the spirits in Hell to come back to Heaven.

A Correct Understanding of Buddha and God

[Chapter 2]
Faith is Wonderful

Which is Correct, Monotheism or Polytheism?

Although people talk of monotheism, In truth there is more than one god

The problem is whether or not there is only one God. If you think there is only one God and the God who came down before you is genuine, then gods who appeared before others must be false. For example, if the God who appeared before the Jewish people in ancient times was the true one, then the God who appeared before others cannot be the true one. Neither can Japanese, Chinese nor Egyptian gods be authentic. If you think, "There is only one God and He watches over only our ethnic group," then naturally, all other gods will appear to be wrong. This way of thinking has produced an enormous amount of hatred and many conflicts throughout human history.

Certainly, when a religion emerges, there is generally one principal guiding spirit with a divine character. A particular spirit may guide people by saying, "Follow my teachings and act accordingly." However, this does not necessarily mean there is no other divinity. There are actually other gods. As you can see, there are so many people in the world. Unless there are many gods, it is impossible to make everyone happy. Many gods share responsibilities and work. And there are also supervising spirits who take overall responsibility in their respective areas.

That is how it works. While Heaven decides who will take charge in starting a religion in a particular age and region, this does not imply that the gods who emerge in other regions and countries are false.

Aside from Yahweh, Elohim [El Cantare] Also appears in the Old Testament

Monotheism that centered on Yahweh provides us with a good example. Yahweh is said to be a jealous god who forbids the worship of other gods. But is Judaism truly monotheistic? Do Jewish people believe in only one God? In fact, when we read the Old Testament, we can see that this is not true. The Old Testament refers to two gods: Yahweh and Elohim. They are two different beings. Yahweh is the god who we now call "Enlil" and in fact, Elohim in the Old Testament means "El Cantare." Both of them are in charge. So you can see, the Old Testament already reveals that there are two gods. Thus, there is not only one God.

At one time, a god who was guiding people might have told those who believed in wrong religions, "Believe in me as the only true God." However, this did not mean that he did not allow other gods to exist. If there are people who really believe in wrong religions, it is of course acceptable to say to them, "Stop worshipping that evil god. Believe only in me." But if it means all other religions are wrong or all other gods are false, this will produce a great deal of confusion.

Multiple spiritual beings guided Muhammad

Islam is another good example of monotheism. The Koran is filled with praise to Allah as the Almighty God. Actually, Muhammad channeled Allah's words as spiritual messages. Interestingly, Allah sometimes refers to himself as "I," and at other times, "we." He frequently uses the plural form, "we." Muslims do not really understand why, so they think "we" is also a name for Allah. However, this means that there was a group of guiding spirits. Even though the representative god called himself Allah, there was a group of guiding spirits who took turns giving various teachings. This is the truth. Therefore, it cannot really be called monotheism.

Even if there is a main spirit in charge, there are other guiding spirits.

What Kind of Being is El Cantare?

El Cantare has the greatest responsibility In the terrestrial spirit group

There is a group of spirits in the terrestrial spirit group who take on a great mission. They are called high spirits and, from the perspective of humans living on earth, some of these high spirits appear so superior that they are sometimes called *gods*. They are called gods in the meaning of "gods who have human characteristics." In contrast, the name *Buddha* originally means "the awakened one" or "the enlightened one." It often refers to Gautama Siddhartha or Shakyamuni Buddha, who had descended to earth, but it also refers to the Primordial Buddha. Primordial Buddha has a meaning that is equivalent to God, the Creator of the Great Universe. This is the basic difference between Buddha and God.

The Grand Spirit that stands above all is called *El Cantare*. And with the greatest authority in the terrestrial spirit group, He has been guiding humanity. El Cantare has been responsible for Earth from time immemorial, before human beings were created. He is a being in whom God and Buddha are united. A part of the consciousness of El Cantare was born in India as Gautama Siddhartha or Shakyamuni Buddha.

The word *El* means "light" and *Cantare* means "land" or "Earth," so El Cantare means "Earth filled with light." As the highest spirit of the terrestrial spirit group, El Cantare has the greatest responsibility and He makes the final decisions regarding the destiny of humankind. Of course, Earth has Grand Spirits other than El Cantare and these Grand Spirits in the ninth dimension are now cooperating to give guidance to Happy Science. Happy Science was established by El Cantare and is working toward creating utopia on Earth. In this sense, it is not an organization established by human beings; Happy Science was created by the consensus of the Grand Spirits who inhabit the great Spirit World surrounding Earth, for the purpose of saving all humankind. The mission of Happy Science is to save all humankind through the dissemination of global and universal Truth taught by El Cantare.

Supreme God of the Earth, El Cantare

Ra Mu
17,000 years ago
Mu continent

Core consciousness
Ryuho Okawa
Present-day
Japan

Gautama Siddhartha
[Shakyamuni Buddha]
2,600 years ago
India

Thoth
12,000 years ago
Atlantis

Hermes
4,300 years ago
Greece

Rient Arl Croud
7,000 years ago
Ancient Incan Empire

Ophealis
6,500 years ago
Greece

On the Supreme God:

There are many god-like spirits in the Spirit World. While "god" is a status, it has different ranks. And the supreme leader in the world of gods is El Cantare.

Happy Science has a grand desire to establish faith in the Supreme God El Cantare and, as a world religion, unite the entire world, even though this may take us hundreds or thousands of years to achieve.

Are There Any Benefits to Joining a Right Religion?

You can receive guidance in The other world after death

Even if you are not really a devout believer, it is better to belong to some kind of religious group or denomination. Generally, the souls of your departed father, mother or relatives will come to guide you after death, but this is not always the case. Sometimes they cannot come because they, themselves, are undergoing training. In such cases, salvation will be somewhat difficult and you may have a hard time, so it is better to belong to some kind of religion.

Even if you do not have faith yourself, if there are some among your friends or those close to you who do have faith, fortunately, you will be able to have some connection to a religion through them.

Upon the death of a friend, a devout person will worry about the departed one and will wholeheartedly perform a memorial service or pray for the dead friend's soul to return to Heaven. Then, the soul will be connected to the devout friend's guardian spirit or the guiding spirit group of the religion that the devout friend belongs to. These spirits will thus commit themselves to guide the dead friend's soul and make the necessary arrangements until the soul's destination in the other world is determined.

When you arrive in the other world, you will have a hard time if there is nobody to guide you.

After death, the soul leaves the body and passes through a tunnel until it comes to a land of light. It then travels through fields of flowers until it arrives at the Styx. In Japan, the border between life and death generally takes the form of a river, though sometimes it can be a lake. In Switzerland, it takes the form of a mountain pass. But whatever the form may be, the soul needs some kind of guide.

That is why religious leaders carry out missionary work in this world to guide people to the Truth. If they fail to guide people in this world, they will continue to do so in the other world. This is something I would like you to know.

There are numerous spirits working in the other world to guide the souls of the departed. The more I see of their actual work, the more I feel just how much care each and every person is treated with.

There are over six billion people living on earth and every day, there are those who die from accidents or illness. This information is transmitted in the appropriate way to the Spirit World and the ones who are connected to the deceased will come to help them. Their friends and relatives, as well as those belonging to religious groups will come to help them. Large numbers of spirits in the other world are informed about people's deaths.

Looking at this, I feel that every single person is treated with great care. I am sure that many are working to make this possible.

Why is Faith Important?

Faith is the last thing that will remain with you

There are many wonderful things in this world, but ultimately you must always be ready to choose faith over all else. You must abandon all worldly things when you depart this world. All that you will be left with is your faith.

In the past, I have preached on countless occasions that when you die and go to the other world, all that will remain with you is your mind. It is true that you will indeed take your mind with you, but as to where you will end up, it could be Heaven or Hell. There are minds destined for Heaven and minds destined for Hell.

That being so, you will lose everything after you die, including your home, wealth, family, friends, possessions, business cards and all other material things. You will lose them all and the only thing you can take with you to the other world will be your mind. Then, if we take this teaching one step further, the only thing that you can take with you when you return to the other world is your faith.

If you have faith, there will be no confusion as to where you will settle when you reach the other world. It is none other than your faith that holds the key to Heaven or the gate to Heaven. Faith is also the requirement for you to live in Heaven. It is also the requirement for you to become an Angel of Light.

Epilogue

Life is Only about a Couple Dozen Thousand Days, So Live in a Way that Will Serve to Improve Your Soul

What is the "happiness" taught at Happy Science? While most happiness theories focus on happiness in this world, happiness theory as taught by Happy Science aims at achieving happiness, not only in earthly terms but also from the viewpoint of the other world. We refer to this happiness as "the happiness that runs through this world and the next."

In other words, I want everyone to live in a way that is filled with happiness, not only in this world but also in the other world. So I advocate a lifestyle that will allow you to continue living happily in the other world as well, after you die. I sincerely hope that you all practice this.

Of course, in reality, there are people who live unhappily in this world and remain unhappy in the other world as well. There are also those who appear to be happy in this world but become unhappy in the next. There are yet others who lead unhappy lives in this world but find great joy after death. Finally, there are those who are happy in this world and happy in the next as well. Simply put, there are four types of people.

I am recommending that you follow the fourth path; that is to say, be happy in this world and happy in the next, too. I recommend what I believe is ultimately the best.

Naturally, there are other ways of thinking. If you have a completely negative view of this world, you will think that even though you may live a miserable life in this world, it does not matter as long as you can find happiness in the next.

Among Christians, there are many who willingly suffer misery and sadness during their lives in the belief that this will bring them happiness in the next world. That is because their master and teacher, Jesus Christ, had a tragic life in this world. Since their master and teacher was a tragic figure, those who follow him have chosen lives of tragedy, pursuing glory and happiness in the other world.

However, I do not necessarily think that this is the best way of living. While we are here for only some decades, I do recognize that our lives on earth have a certain meaning. Humans are not simply repeating actions that are completely meaningless.

My basic philosophy is this: "People are born into this world because there is a reason for them to do so. During the decades of life, they have a role to play and a purpose to fulfill. People are born into this world in order to learn something and, after they have done this, they take it back with them to the Real World, to the true world they originally came from."

For this reason, I do not completely deny this world. I admit that this world is an extremely important place where people can train, educate and refine their souls. I am saying that gaining a lot of nourishment for the soul and experiencing joy in this world represent a very happy way of life. This way of life will also lead you to happiness in the other world.

You may feel that a life of seven or eight decades is a long time, but if you translate this into days, it means that you are only here for a couple dozen thousand days or so on average. You may have imagined that your life would last one or two hundred thousand days, but in fact you only live for a couple dozen thousand days.

Each day passes like the sand in an hourglass. After 20,000 to 30,000 days, the day will come when you have to leave this world. Thought of in this way, life on earth is indeed extremely short.

During these roughly 20,000 days, how much will you experience and how much Truth will you be able to grasp? This is an extremely important point. Humans lead their lives on earth to gain such precious experience.

It is for this purpose that you are born as a baby into this world, study in school, become an adult and work, get married and raise a family. You will get old in this way, sometimes experiencing sickness, until eventually you leave this world.

You are only here for around 20,000 days. How will you make this an ideal life, so that it serves to improve your soul when you return to the other world? This is the extremely important issue.

Afterword

This book is ideal for those who are coming in contact with the world of religion for the very first time. It encompasses all kinds of spiritual knowledge and can be described as one of the best textbooks for you to step forward courageously into the wonderland called the spiritual world.

I sincerely hope that the contents of this book will become "the common knowledge of the 21st century."

Ryuho Okawa
Founder and CEO of the Happy Science Group
September 2009

ABOUT THE AUTHOR

Founder and CEO of Happy Science Group.

Ryuho Okawa was born on July 7th 1956, in Tokushima, Japan. After graduating from the University of Tokyo with a law degree, he joined a Tokyo-based trading house. While working at its New York headquarters, he studied international finance at the Graduate Center of the City University of New York. In 1981, he attained Great Enlightenment and became aware that he is El Cantare with a mission to bring salvation to all humankind.

In 1986, he established Happy Science. It now has members in over 165 countries across the world, with more than 700 branches and temples as well as 10,000 missionary houses around the world.

He has given over 3,450 lectures (of which more than 150 are in English) and published over 3,000 books (of which more than 600 are Spiritual Interview Series), and many are translated into 40 languages. Along with *The Laws of the Sun* and *The Laws Of Messiah*, many of the books have become best sellers or million sellers. To date, Happy Science has produced 25 movies. The original story and original concept were given by the Executive Producer Ryuho Okawa. He has also composed music and written lyrics of over 450 pieces.

Moreover, he is the Founder of Happy Science University and Happy Science Academy (Junior and Senior High School), Founder and President of the Happiness Realization Party, Founder and Honorary Headmaster of Happy Science Institute of Government and Management, Founder of IRH Press Co., Ltd., and the Chairperson of NEW STAR PRODUCTION Co., Ltd. and ARI Production Co., Ltd.

WHAT IS EL CANTARE?

El Cantare means "the Light of the Earth," and is the Supreme God of the Earth who has been guiding humankind since the beginning of Genesis. He is whom Jesus called Father and Muhammad called Allah, and is *Ame-no-Mioya-Gami*, Japanese Father God. Different parts of El Cantare's core consciousness have descended to Earth in the past, once as Alpha and another as Elohim. His branch spirits, such as Shakyamuni Buddha and Hermes, have descended to Earth many times and helped to flourish many civilizations. To unite various religions and to integrate various fields of study in order to build a new civilization on Earth, a part of the core consciousness has descended to Earth as Master Ryuho Okawa.

Alpha is a part of the core consciousness of El Cantare who descended to Earth around 330 million years ago. Alpha preached Earth's Truths to harmonize and unify Earth-born humans and space people who came from other planets.

Elohim is a part of El Cantare's core consciousness who descended to Earth around 150 million years ago. He gave wisdom, mainly on the differences of light and darkness, good and evil.

Ame-no-Mioya-Gami (Japanese Father God) is the Creator God and the Father God who appears in the ancient literature, *Hotsuma Tsutae*. It is believed that He descended on the foothills of Mt. Fuji about 30,000 years ago and built the Fuji dynasty, which is the root of the Japanese civilization. With justice as the central pillar, Ame-no-Mioya-Gami's teachings spread to ancient civilizations of other countries in the world.

Shakyamuni Buddha was born as a prince into the Shakya Clan in India around 2,600 years ago. When he was 29 years old, he renounced the world and sought enlightenment. He later attained Great Enlightenment and founded Buddhism.

Hermes is one of the 12 Olympian gods in Greek mythology, but the spiritual Truth is that he taught the teachings of love and progress around 4,300 years ago that became the origin of the current Western civilization. He is a hero that truly existed.

Ophealis was born in Greece around 6,500 years ago and was the leader who took an expedition to as far as Egypt. He is the God of miracles, prosperity, and arts, and is known as Osiris in the Egyptian mythology.

Rient Arl Croud was born as a king of the ancient Incan Empire around 7,000 years ago and taught about the mysteries of the mind. In the heavenly world, he is responsible for the interactions that take place between various planets.

Thoth was an almighty leader who built the golden age of the Atlantic civilization around 12,000 years ago. In the Egyptian mythology, he is known as god Thoth.

Ra Mu was a leader who built the golden age of the civilization of Mu around 17,000 years ago. As a religious leader and a politician, he ruled by uniting religion and politics.

ABOUT HAPPY SCIENCE

Happy Science is a global movement that empowers individuals to find purpose and spiritual happiness and to share that happiness with their families, societies, and the world. With more than 12 million members around the world, Happy Science aims to increase awareness of spiritual truths and expand our capacity for love, compassion, and joy so that together we can create the kind of world we all wish to live in.

Activities at Happy Science are based on the Principle of Happiness (Love, Wisdom, Self-Reflection, and Progress). This principle embraces worldwide philosophies and beliefs, transcending boundaries of culture and religions.

Love teaches us to give ourselves freely without expecting anything in return; it encompasses giving, nurturing, and forgiving.

Wisdom leads us to the insights of spiritual truths, and opens us to the true meaning of life and the will of God (the universe, the highest power, Buddha).

Self-Reflection brings a mindful, nonjudgmental lens to our thoughts and actions to help us find our truest selves—the essence of our souls—and deepen our connection to the highest power. It helps us attain a clean and peaceful mind and leads us to the right life path.

Progress emphasizes the positive, dynamic aspects of our spiritual growth—actions we can take to manifest and spread happiness around the world. It's a path that not only expands our soul growth, but also furthers the collective potential of the world we live in.

PROGRAMS AND EVENTS

The doors of Happy Science are open to all. We offer a variety of programs and events, including self-exploration and self-growth programs, spiritual seminars, meditation and contemplation sessions, study groups, and book events.

Our programs are designed to:
* Deepen your understanding of your purpose and meaning in life
* Improve your relationships and increase your capacity to love unconditionally
* Attain peace of mind, decrease anxiety and stress, and feel positive
* Gain deeper insights and a broader perspective on the world
* Learn how to overcome life's challenges
    ... and much more.

For more information, visit <u>happy-science.org</u>.

OUR ACTIVITIES

Happy Science does other various activities to provide support for those in need.

◆ **You Are An Angel! General Incorporated Association**

Happy Science has a volunteer network in Japan that encourages and supports children with disabilities as well as their parents and guardians.

◆ **Never Mind School for Truancy**

At 'Never Mind,' we support students who find it very challenging to attend schools in Japan. We also nurture their self-help spirit and power to rebound against obstacles in life based on Master Okawa's teachings and faith.

◆ **"Prevention Against Suicide" Campaign since 2003**

A nationwide campaign to reduce suicides; over 20,000 people commit suicide every year in Japan. "The Suicide Prevention Website-Words of Truth for You-" presents spiritual prescriptions for worries such as depression, lost love, extramarital affairs, bullying and work-related problems, thereby saving many lives.

◆ **Support for Anti-bullying Campaigns**

Happy Science provides support for a group of parents and guardians, Network to Protect Children from Bullying, a general incorporated foundation launched in Japan to end bullying, including those that can even be called a criminal offense. So far, the network received more than 5,000 cases and resolved 90% of them.

- **The Golden Age Scholarship**

This scholarship is granted to students who can contribute greatly and bring a hopeful future to the world.

- **Success No.1**
Buddha's Truth Afterschool Academy

Happy Science has over 180 classrooms throughout Japan and in several cities around the world that focus on afterschool education for children. The education focuses on faith and morals in addition to supporting children's school studies.

- **Angel Plan V**

For children under the age of kindergarten, Happy Science holds classes for nurturing healthy, positive, and creative boys and girls.

- **Future Stars Training Department**

The Future Stars Training Department was founded within the Happy Science Media Division with the goal of nurturing talented individuals to become successful in the performing arts and entertainment industry.

- **NEW STAR PRODUCTION Co., Ltd.**
ARI Production Co., Ltd.

We have companies to nurture actors and actresses, artists, and vocalists. They are also involved in film production.

CONTACT INFORMATION

Happy Science is a worldwide organization with branches and temples around the globe. For a comprehensive list, visit the worldwide directory at *happy-science.org*. The following are some of the many Happy Science locations:

UNITED STATES AND CANADA

New York
79 Franklin St., New York, NY 10013, USA
Phone: 1-212-343-7972
Fax: 1-212-343-7973
Email: ny@happy-science.org
Website: happyscience-usa.org

New Jersey
66 Hudson St., #2R, Hoboken, NJ 07030, USA
Phone: 1-201-313-0127
Email: nj@happy-science.org
Website: happyscience-usa.org

Chicago
2300 Barrington Rd., Suite #400,
Hoffman Estates, IL 60169, USA
Phone: 1-630-937-3077
Email: chicago@happy-science.org
Website: happyscience-usa.org

Florida
5208 8th St., Zephyrhills, FL 33542, USA
Phone: 1-813-715-0000
Fax: 1-813-715-0010
Email: florida@happy-science.org
Website: happyscience-usa.org

Atlanta
1874 Piedmont Ave., NE Suite 360-C
Atlanta, GA 30324, USA
Phone: 1-404-892-7770
Email: atlanta@happy-science.org
Website: happyscience-usa.org

San Francisco
525 Clinton St.
Redwood City, CA 94062, USA
Phone & Fax: 1-650-363-2777
Email: sf@happy-science.org
Website: happyscience-usa.org

Los Angeles
1590 E. Del Mar Blvd., Pasadena, CA
91106, USA
Phone: 1-626-395-7775
Fax: 1-626-395-7776
Email: la@happy-science.org
Website: happyscience-usa.org

Orange County
16541 Gothard St. Suite 104
Huntington Beach, CA 92647
Phone: 1-714-659-1501
Email: oc@happy-science.org
Website: happyscience-usa.org

San Diego
7841 Balboa Ave. Suite #202
San Diego, CA 92111, USA
Phone: 1-626-395-7775
Fax: 1-626-395-7776
E-mail: sandiego@happy-science.org
Website: happyscience-usa.org

Hawaii
Phone: 1-808-591-9772
Fax: 1-808-591-9776
Email: hi@happy-science.org
Website: happyscience-usa.org

Kauai
3343 Kanakolu Street, Suite 5
Lihue, HI 96766, USA
Phone: 1-808-822-7007
Fax: 1-808-822-6007
Email: kauai-hi@happy-science.org
Website: happyscience-usa.org

Toronto
845 The Queensway
Etobicoke, ON M8Z 1N6, Canada
Phone: 1-416-901-3747
Email: toronto@happy-science.org
Website: happy-science.ca

Vancouver
#201-2607 East 49th Avenue,
Vancouver, BC, V5S 1J9, Canada
Phone: 1-604-437-7735
Fax: 1-604-437-7764
Email: vancouver@happy-science.org
Website: happy-science.ca

INTERNATIONAL

Tokyo
1-6-7 Togoshi, Shinagawa,
Tokyo, 142-0041, Japan
Phone: 81-3-6384-5770
Fax: 81-3-6384-5776
Email: tokyo@happy-science.org
Website: happy-science.org

Seoul
74, Sadang-ro 27-gil,
Dongjak-gu, Seoul, Korea
Phone: 82-2-3478-8777
Fax: 82-2-3478-9777
Email: korea@happy-science.org
Website: happyscience-korea.org

London
3 Margaret St.
London, W1W 8RE United Kingdom
Phone: 44-20-7323-9255
Fax: 44-20-7323-9344
Email: eu@happy-science.org
Website: www.happyscience-uk.org

Taipei
No. 89, Lane 155, Dunhua N. Road,
Songshan District, Taipei City 105, Taiwan
Phone: 886-2-2719-9377
Fax: 886-2-2719-5570
Email: taiwan@happy-science.org
Website: happyscience-tw.org

Sydney
516 Pacific Highway, Lane Cove North,
2066 NSW, Australia
Phone: 61-2-9411-2877
Fax: 61-2-9411-2822
Email: sydney@happy-science.org

Kuala Lumpur
No 22A, Block 2, Jalil Link Jalan Jalil
Jaya 2, Bukit Jalil 57000,
Kuala Lumpur, Malaysia
Phone: 60-3-8998-7877
Fax: 60-3-8998-7977
Email: malaysia@happy-science.org
Website: happyscience.org.my

Sao Paulo
Rua. Domingos de Morais 1154,
Vila Mariana, Sao Paulo SP
CEP 04010-100, Brazil
Phone: 55-11-5088-3800
Email: sp@happy-science.org
Website: happyscience.com.br

Kathmandu
Kathmandu Metropolitan City,
Ward No. 15, Ring Road, Kimdol,
Sitapaila Kathmandu, Nepal
Phone: 977-1-427-2931
Email: nepal@happy-science.org

Jundiai
Rua Congo, 447, Jd. Bonfiglioli
Jundiai-CEP, 13207-340, Brazil
Phone: 55-11-4587-5952
Email: jundiai@happy-science.org

Kampala
Plot 877 Rubaga Road, Kampala
P.O. Box 34130 Kampala, UGANDA
Phone: 256-79-4682-121
Email: uganda@happy-science.org

ABOUT HAPPINESS REALIZATION PARTY

The Happiness Realization Party (HRP) was founded in May 2009 by Master Ryuho Okawa as part of the Happy Science Group. HRP strives to improve the Japanese society, based on three basic political principles of "freedom, democracy, and faith," and let Japan promote individual and public happiness from Asia to the world as a leader nation.

1) Diplomacy and Security: Protecting Freedom, Democracy, and Faith of Japan and the World from China's Totalitarianism

Japan's current defense system is insufficient against China's expanding hegemony and the threat of North Korea's nuclear missiles. Japan, as the leader of Asia, must strengthen its defense power and promote strategic diplomacy together with the nations which share the values of freedom, democracy, and faith. Further, HRP aims to realize world peace under the leadership of Japan, the nation with the spirit of religious tolerance.

2) Economy: Early economic recovery through utilizing the "wisdom of the private sector"

Economy has been damaged severely by the novel coronavirus originated in China. Many companies have been forced into bankruptcy or out of business. What is needed for economic recovery now is not subsidies and regulations by the government, but policies which can utilize the "wisdom of the private sector."

For more information, visit en.hr-party.jp

ABOUT HS PRESS

HS Press is an imprint of IRH Press Co., Ltd. IRH Press Co., Ltd., based in Tokyo, was founded in 1987 as a publishing division of Happy Science. IRH Press publishes religious and spiritual books, journals, magazines and also operates broadcast and film production enterprises. For more information, visit *okawabooks.com*.

Follow us on:

f Facebook: Okawa Books   ⊙ Instagram: OkawaBooks

▶ Youtube: Okawa Books   🐦 Twitter: Okawa Books

𝓟 Pinterest: Okawa Books   g Goodreads: Ryuho Okawa

――――― **NEWSLETTER** ―――――

To receive book related news, promotions and events, please subscribe to our newsletter below.

🔗 eepurl.com/bsMeJj

――――― **AUDIO / VISUAL MEDIA** ―――――

YOUTUBE

PODCAST

Introduction of Ryuho Okawa's titles; topics ranging from self-help, current affairs, spirituality, religion, and the universe.

BOOKS BY RYUHO OKAWA

The Laws of Wisdom
Shine Your Diamond Within

ISBN: 978-1941779361
$14.95 (Paperback)

An invitation to intellectual happiness, which is filled with infinite possibilities.

The Laws of Wisdom guides you along the path on how to acquire wisdom, so that you can break through any wall you are or will confront in your life or in your business. By reading this book, you will be able to avoid getting lost in the flood of information and, going beyond the level of just amassing knowledge, be able to come up with many great ideas, make effective planning and strategy and develop your leadership while receiving good inspiration.

Let's all break through walls, open up a path and create a bright future!

BASICS OF EXORCISM

HOW TO PROTECT YOU AND YOUR FAMILY
FROM EVIL SPIRITS

ISBN: 978-1941779347
$14.95 (Paperback)

The truth regarding spiritual disturbance and the technique to cope with demons and evil spirits:
- Science and medicine are yet to give answers
- Existing religions give insufficient explanations

No matter how much time progresses, demons are real. Unhappiness and misfortune in life caused by possession. Spiritual background behind schizophrenia and multiple personality.
Spiritual screen against curses - the truth of exorcism as told by the author who possesses the six great supernatural powers -

The essence of exorcism as a result of more than 5000 rounds of exorcist experience!

THE LAWS OF GREAT ENLIGHTENMENT

Always Walk with Buddha

ISBN: 978-1-941779-28-6
$14.95 (Paperback)

Buddhist Approaches to Become Stress-Free

In this modern society, people tend to live a stressful life and experience hurting others or being hurt by others. Often they find themselves unable to forgive someone, making it difficult for them to maintain a peaceful mind. However, there are ways to lead a stress-free life and enjoy happiness from within.

This book offers you the practical approaches to achieve it. By understanding the Buddhist concept "enlightenment" described here, you will gain the power to forgive sins and get to know how to be the master of your own mind, not a slave to your emotions.

After reading this book, your view of the world will completely change, and come to understand that we are living in a beautiful world that God created.

INTO THE STORM OF
INTERNATIONAL POLITICS
THE NEW STANDARDS OF THE WORLD ORDER

ISBN: 978-1941779279
$14.95 (Paperback)

In September 2013, President Obama stated, "We should not be the world's policeman." As signified by those words, America has been declining and the world order is being lost. In the Middle East, Islamic State declared independence in June 2014. Furthermore, in Hong Kong, the Umbrella Revolution - a movement against China's anti-democratic, single-party dictatorship - broke out in September 2014.

At the roots of these three movements lie three different sets of values. America's decline indicates Christian civilization not having clear standards on what justice is in this complex world of the current era. The problem with Islamic State is that a portion of Muslims in the current era have lost the spirit of peace and tolerance that Muhammad taught. Totalitarianism of China is founded upon materialism, a thought which denies human dignity and freedom of the individual. The world is now seeking a new idea or a new philosophy that will show the countries with such values the direction they should head in.

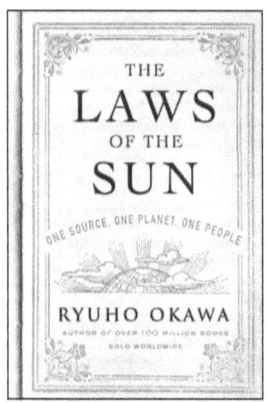

THE LAWS OF THE SUN
ONE SOURCE, ONE PLANET, ONE PEOPLE

ISBN: 978-1-937673-04-8
$24.95 (Hardcover)

IMAGINE IF YOU COULD ASK GOD why He created this world and what spiritual laws He used to shape us—and everything around us. If we could understand His designs and intentions, we could discover what our goals in life should be and whether our actions move us closer to those goals or farther away.

At a young age, a spiritual calling prompted Ryuho Okawa to outline what he innately understood to be universal truths for all humankind. In The Laws of the Sun, Okawa outlines these laws of the universe and provides a road map for living one's life with greater purpose and meaning.

In this powerful book, Ryuho Okawa reveals the transcendent nature of consciousness and the secrets of our multidimensional universe and our place in it. By understanding the different stages of love and following the Buddhist Eightfold Path, he believes we can speed up our eternal process of development. The Laws of the Sun shows the way to realize true happiness—a happiness that continues from this world through the other.

THE NINE DIMENSIONS
UNVEILING THE LAWS OF ETERNITY

ISBN: 978-0-9826985-6-3
$15.95 (Paperback)

THIS BOOK IS YOUR GATE TO HEAVEN. In this book, Master Okawa shows that God designed this world and the vast, wondrous world of our afterlife as a school with many levels through which our souls learn and grow. This book is a window into the mind of our loving God, who encourages us to grow into greater angels.

Also by Ryuho Okawa

THE SCIENCE OF HAPPINESS
10 Principles for Manifesting Your Divine Nature

THE GOLDEN LAWS
History through the Eyes of the Eternal Buddha

THE STARTING POINT OF HAPPINESS
A Practical and Intuitive Guide to
Discovering Love, Wisdom, and Faith

LOVE, NURTURE, AND FORGIVE
A Handbook to Add a New Richness to Your Life

AN UNSHAKABLE MIND
How to Overcome Life's Difficulties

THE ORIGIN OF LOVE
On the Beauty of Compassion

INVINCIBLE THINKING
There Is No Such Thing as Defeat

GUIDEPOSTS TO HAPPINESS
Prescriptions for a Wonderful Life

THE LAWS OF HAPPINESS
The Four Principles for a Successful Life

TIPS TO FIND HAPPINESS
Creating a Harmonious Home for
Your Spouse, Your Children, and Yourself

THE PHILOSOPHY OF PROGRESS
Higher Thinking for Developing Infinite Prosperity

THE ESSENCE OF BUDDHA
The Path to Enlightenment

THE CHALLENGE OF THE MIND
A Practical Approach to the Essential Buddhist Teaching of Karma

THE CHALLENGE OF ENLIGHTENMENT
Realize Your Inner Potential

THE MANIFESTO OF THE HAPPINESS REALIZATION PARTY

RYUHO OKAWA: A POLITICAL REVOLUTIONARY
The Originator of Abenomics and Father of the Happiness Realization Party

SPIRITUAL MESSAGES FROM THE GUARDIAN SPIRIT OF RYUHO OKAWA
The Divine Voice of Shakyamuni Buddha

THE IMPORTANCE OF THE EXPLORATION OF THE RIGHT MIND

INTO THE STORM OF INTERNATIONAL POLITICS
The New Standards of the World Order

Higher Education Series

THE NEW IDEA OF A UNIVERSITY
The Groundbreaking Mission of Happy Science University

THE BASIC TEACHINGS OF HAPPY SCIENCE
A Happiness Theory on Truth and Faith

Spiritual Interview Series

IN LOVE WITH THE SUN
SPIRITUAL MESSAGES FROM GODDESS GAIA

Ryuho Okawa & Shio Okawa

ISBN: 978-1-941779-26-2
$14.95 (Paperback)

After 600 million years, people shall know the true genesis.

The true story when the earth was born, The guiding concept of the earth, The mechanism of creating life on Earth. And the future that human beings has to seek, These secrets are now revealed by the spiritual message from Goddess Gaia, Who supported the creation of Earth civilization by Alpha, the God of origin.

Through reading this book, you will see the magnificent scale of El Cantare's Law.

"I would like for you to listen to the bell ringing the advent of a spiritual revolution."

— Ryuho Okawa, Preface

THE TRUTH OF THE PACIFIC WAR
SOULFUL MESSAGES FROM HIDEKI TOJO,
JAPAN'S WARTIME LEADER

ISBN: 978-1-941779-22-4
$14.95 (Paperback)

In this book, we provide you with the material needed to rethink whether or not the perception of World War II by the winners was right, through looking back on history starting with the current world affairs. This is all necessary for us to get a thorough understanding of ongoing confusion in the world and to seek the path of peace, stability and progress of future humankind.

The material provided is a new testimony by General Hideki Tojo, who is enshrined at Yasukuni Shrine and who was Japan's most significant figure in the Pacific War. Furthermore, we have also recorded a testimony by Supreme Commander of the Allied Powers Douglas MacArthur in order to ensure a fair argument.

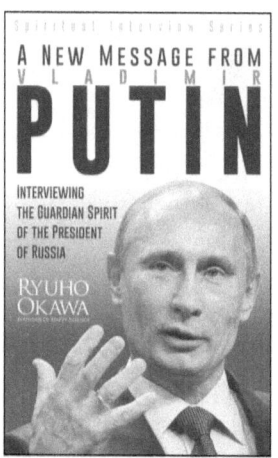

A NEW MESSAGE FROM VLADIMIR PUTIN

INTERVIEWING THE GUARDIAN SPIRIT OF
THE PRESIDENT OF RUSSIA

ISBN: 978-1-937673-94-9
$14.95 (Paperback)

We hereby bring you the most recent spiritual message from the guardian spirit of President Putin, the politician who is the center of attention of not just the people of Russia but of the whole world, regardless of it being in a good or a bad way. In the Preface, it says, "President Putin's true intentions, which are 90 percent misunderstood."

We hope that, through this book, the reader will come to understand the true thoughts of Mr. Putin which are still undisclosed to the public. And, we hope that the reader will foresee the new world order that this skilled politician is thinking of, and make use of that in predicting how the international affairs will turn out in the future.

THE GENIUS OF ICHIRO
The Secret Behind His Four Thousand Hits

ISBN: 978-1-941779-04-0
$14.95 (Paperback)

Ichiro Suzuki arrived in Seattle in 2001 as a mostly anonymous free agent from Japan's NPB, and while there was buzz about his potential, no one really knew what to expect. Since then, he has set many records in American Major League Baseball, including the record for most hits in a single season (262) and longest streak of two-hundred-hit seasons (ten years). On August 21, 2013, he got the four thousandth hit of his professional baseball career. This spiritual interview reveals the "making of Ichiro," including the secrets to his professionalism, his techniques for overcoming slumps, and how he made it to the top. The interview highlights Ichiro's unique traits that continue to impress us, twelve years after he first unleashed the laser beam.

ON HAPPINESS REVOLUTION
A SPIRITUAL INTERVIEW WITH HANNAH ARENDT

ISBN: 978-1-937673-82-6
$14.95 (Paperback)

Since 2010, Master Ryuho Okawa has published over two hundred spiritual messages, in Japanese, from the spirits of historical men and women and the guardian spirits of today's living figures. With this Spiritual Interview Series, Master Okawa is now making these important messages available in English. The books in this series are messages from the spirits or guardian spirits of people who have a great deal of influence over world affairs. These messages reveal these powerful figures' hidden intentions and disclose facts that even news reporters would have difficulty drawing out. Master Okawa's in-depth analyses of these messages give us the tools that we need to understand and confront the dangers that lie ahead of us. Master Okawa hopes to show readers that the spirit world and spirits are real, and that by understanding spiritual truths, we can bring a peaceful end to international conflicts and create solutions to a variety of global crises.

For a complete list of books in the Spiritual Interview Series, visit spiritualinterview.com